Leadership
A Quick and Easy Guide

by Barbara Birkett, Warren Daum, and Miles Southworth

"It has become increasingly evident to me that whenever significant change occurs in our society, the operative word is *leadership*. Be it a business, a school or a municipality, change occurs when a person equipped with the skills of a leader causes that change to happen. Peel away the layers surrounding substantive change, for good or bad, and inevitably at the center is a 'leader.'"

"The recognition of this fact can cause friction because leadership is so often seen or described in amorphous terms, as something difficult to grasp or define. It therefore seems elusive."

"This book counters that point of view. *Leadership: A Quick and Easy Guide* is just that. It accesses the components of leadership quickly, directly, and in an easy-to-read fashion. It makes the concept of leadership reachable. It therefore provides a real public service."

DANIEL L. BRATTON, President
The Chautauqua Institution

"Birkett, Daum and Southworth in *Leadership: A Quick and Easy Guide* simplify the large body of research and writing on leadership with an acute use of common sense. For leaders in business and community associations intent on improvement or those who just want to be better citizens, the book will be located within easy reach. Assessment and other devices invite the user's notes and experiences, and can make the book one's own."

PAUL A MILLER,
President Emeritus
Rochester Institute of Technology

"This is a good book, something for everyone. It offers a solution for many situations and warrants a read through. It is worthy of a spot on your reference shelf."

GEORGE RYAN, President
GATF/NASF

"If we wish to insure the safety, security and quality of our future world, then the key is to prepare a superb cadre of leaders. This wonderful book adds to the arsenal of leadership resources."

DR. J. MICHAEL ADAMS, Dean
Drexel University

"Leadership should be part of the curriculum for every college student and business manager. This book defines the why and how of this elusive subject as well as any source I have seen."

FRED ROGERS, Managing Director
Research and Engineering Council
of the Graphic Arts Industry

Leadership

A Quick and Easy Guide

Barbara Birkett
Warren Daum
Miles Southworth

Graphic Arts Publishing Inc.
Livonia, New York

To our students, readers, and all those who enthusiastically and responsibly take on leadership roles.

Philosophies

that stand the test of

Time

emerge as universal

Truths.

Table of Contents

Notes

Notes

Notes

Quotation

*And the heaviest penalty
for declining to rule
is to be ruled by someone inferior to yourself.*

From *Republic* by Plato (427 - 347 B.C.)

Our Paraphrase

*And the heaviest penalty
for declining to **lead**
is to be **lead** by someone inferior to yourself.*

Preface

Thousands of words have been written and hundreds of books published on the topics of Leadership, Management, Organization, etc. Then, *why write another book?*

The answer is that we seek to fill what we see as a void—a book that quickly and easily provides a condensed guide to effective leadership. We intend this book to be an easy, yet thought-provoking, read.

Despite the ever-changing world, the basics of leadership have not changed. Leaders develop a set of skills and traits that make them successful. That's what this book is about.

Because you will be called upon—as are most people—at various times in your life to exercise leadership, this type of book can be very helpful, perhaps even essential.

In the book, we discuss the basic skills and traits found well-developed in recognized leaders. Though some of us have more leadership aptitude than others, we believe that leadership can be developed; leadership is an ongoing process. We hope that you treat this book as a "living reference" in which you make notes and jot down ideas and thoughts in the sidebars provided on each page. We have included *Leadership Tips* after each topic to suggest useful ideas that will help you perfect your skills.

In Section IV is a *Personal Leadership Assessment* that we suggest you first take before reading the book to take inventory of your own skills and traits. Next read the book, work for three months on the areas you've identified as needing effort, and then do another assessment. Repeat the process frequently to maintain momentum in developing leadership skills and traits. If you keep this book within ready reach and use it frequently, we will have accomplished our goal. So will you.

We are particularly indebted to our students and colleagues who have provided us with their input and experiences related to many of the topics discussed in the following pages. Special thanks are due to Adelle Wolf for the drawings that appear on selected pages, to JoAnna Daum for library research, and to Donna Southworth for editing assistance. Thanks are also due to our spouses, Bill Birkett, Joan Daum, and Donna Southworth for their understanding and support through repeated meetings and revisions over more years than we wish to admit. Finally, any errors or omissions are solely the authors' responsibility.

Barbara Birkett
Warren Daum
Miles Southworth

Rochester, NY 1999

Section I

Preeminent Leadership Skills and Traits

Notes

Let's Begin

A leader is a person who
- **Envisions**
    - **Engages**
        - **Enables**
            - **Energizes**
individuals to meet objectives by undertaking appropriate actions. These **Four Es** result in **Enacting**, the team's movement toward a goal (see Figure 1).

It is your role as the leader to set and guide the course, to **envision** the future for the organization, department, division, etc. Although *vision is not a voting issue,* input from colleagues and followers is vital, for without followers who buy into your vision, there is no leadership!

Vision is not a voting issue.

Before you can lead, you must have followers to lead. We call this the need to **engage** individuals so that they want to be involved, a bringing together of a team. You cannot expect a team to materialize suddenly, highly motivated, and ready to get started. You usually have some selling, some persuading to do to convince potential followers of the worthiness of your vision. You have to consider the skills and character traits that are needed and then identify people

Notes

who have these skills and traits. These are the people that you need to **engage** in the effort.

Individuals who buy into your vision need to have the resources, skills, financial support, etc. to allow them to embrace it. Here, you must be the **enabler.** Sometimes enabling simply means getting out of the way and letting followers take the initiative. Other times it means direct involvement, such as providing training or reorganizing workflow.

Along with enabling, you will be called upon to **energize,** to show vividly the desirability of the goal, whatever it is—a new organizational structure, a new process, a new product. You need to make clear the benefit of reaching the goal and to create the sustaining desire "to go for it." Energizing, or motivating, is done in specifics with individuals, for each person needs to garner a sense of "what's in it for me" (WIIFM).

There we have it: **Envisioning, Engaging, Enabling,** and **Energizing.** What remains? **Action!** Nothing happens without action. Some call this implementation. We call it **Enacting.** You as leader see the goal, the destination, and the path to it. You are responsible for keeping the goal in sight and for preventing the team from becoming embroiled in useless diversions.

The Five Es of Leadership

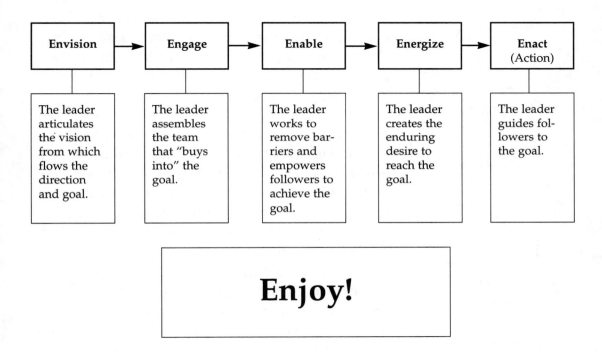

Envision	Engage	Enable	Energize	Enact (Action)
The leader articulates the vision from which flows the direction and goal.	The leader assembles the team that "buys into" the goal.	The leader works to remove barriers and empowers followers to achieve the goal.	The leader creates the enduring desire to reach the goal.	The leader guides followers to the goal.

Enjoy!

Figure 1: Leadership requires effort in all of the Five Es. You need to develop skills that can be applied in each one of these areas. Most skills are applicable in all of the boxes although the degree of applicability and use varies.

Notes

Leadership is a process

The **Five Es** are your roles: **to envision, to engage, to enable, to energize,** and finally, then, **to enact** (see Figure 1), and, we hope, to **enjoy!**

Take just a moment to look ahead in this book through page 41. All of the skills and traits covered to that point are essential to leadership. They occupy a preeminent place in the ability to lead. As you seek to develop leadership ability, you must pay close attention to these.

We use the metaphor of a toolbox to illustrate the idea that as a leader you need many other skills and traits in varying degrees, depending on the demands of the situation. Just as the craftsperson selects the right tool for a job, the leader—having developed a well-inventoried toolbox—can draw upon the appropriate skill or trait as needed by the situation. *Skills can be learned, and traits developed.* For most people, leadership is not an inborn ability. It is a process and it can be learned, and like learning any skill, it requires practice. . . and more practice!

This book identifies the abilities and qualities essential to a leader, and then goes on to identify other skills and traits that are helpful and even essential depending on the situation. All of these attributes are within the reach of the average person. Some are already in your toolbox.

At the very outset, we must point out that leading is built on a mutual trust and respect between the leader and the followers. The leader's actions and words must be congruent; followers must know they can depend on the leader's word. Likewise, the leader must trust the followers. (Read the section, *Honesty, Morality, Integrity.*) Mutual trust sets the stage for effective communication, teambuilding, motivating, and literally for all the factors of leadership. Remember that trust and respect are earned; they cannot be forced upon followers. Although they are usually established over a period of time, they can quickly and easily be destroyed by actions that may seem small but are significant nonetheless: a convenient lie or a failure to keep a promise.

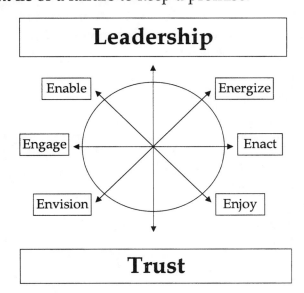

Notes

Trust underpins leadership

Notes

The following pages discuss skills and traits in as few words as possible, for this is to be a *quick and easy leadership guide.* We encourage you to think about each of the topics in relationship to yourself. Try to evaluate how well you have learned and developed each talent. Be proud of those in which you already excel, and pinpoint those which you can improve.

We encourage you to take the *Personal Leadership Assessment* that begins on page 106. Be brutally honest with yourself. Take note of those areas in which you need to improve, read the book and begin to work on those areas by applying suggestions from the book and your own initiatives. Retake the assessment in about three months. The objective is to focus your efforts to develop leadership skills and traits.

Leadership Skills and Traits

Trust
(Fundamental to the leader-follower relationship)

Preeminent Skills and Traits
Vision
Communication
Listening Effectively
Goal Setting/Establishing Priorities
Entrepreneurship/Risk Taking
Motivation
Teambuilding
Commitment
Responsibility/Authority
Initiative

"The Toolbox" of Skills and Traits
Perspective
Fiscal Responsibility
Enthusiasm
Attitude
Observation/Perception
Problem Solving
Networking
Competence
Confidence and Poise
Patience and Persistence
Time Management
Dealing with Frustration and Emotions
Dealing with Stress and Fatigue
Learning from Failure
Heart/Human Relations
Self-Renewal
Self-Esteem
Honesty, Integrity, Morality
Humor

Notes

Vision

People who have vision are able to project themselves into the future and see a happening. That happening or event could be a new or transformed business organization, service or product. To **envision** is the ability to take what you know today and perceive how the world's forces and actions will set the stage for a later event. You might think that to envision is to dream—maybe so, but the vision is a realistic dream. Its roots are based in current events and technology. What is available now is transformed into the new product or service. A visionary conceives a plan of action and is dedicated to making "it" happen.

The leader and a manager have different responsibilities. The leader must provide the insight for the organization. He/She creates the vision and sets the goals. The leader sees ahead to where he/she wants to be, determines the

state of things as they currently are, and formulates a plan to reach the goal.

The manager bears the responsibility for carrying out the policies and strategies necessary to accomplish the vision. The manager

Vision is the leader's responsibility

follows orders and directs the plan to reach the goal. It's important to note that managers can become leaders as they develop their ability to envision.

Through participatory management, the leader may ask individuals to help develop the plan, but the leader probably already knows what strategies will work. Having individuals integrally take part in developing the plan helps them buy ownership in it. Therefore the project is more likely to succeed.

Vision is necessary to progress to the cutting edge of technology or current business strategies. Without foresight, we are always in a catch-up mode behind the competition. A "me-too" strategy does not set the stage for great success. At best, it is a survival strategy.

Both managers and followers are needed to carry out the plan. However, it is more challenging and exciting to be the person setting the course. In the words of Lee Ioccoca, "You have to lead, follow, or get out of the way."

Notes

Notes

Leadership Tips

1. Keep abreast of technologies that impact your industry or area. Read magazines voraciously; attend conferences, expositions and seminars.

2. Read books, magazines and other material from a broad selection. Many of the important paradigm changes that affect an industry occur outside of it. Try to gain as broad a perspective as possible.

3. Listen carefully—to futurists, to followers, to competitors.

4. Take time to think! Note trends. Analyze available information: financials by product, by geographic area, etc. Note changes in the work force.

5. Network with people. Join a group(s), not necessarily in your industry, in which smart people share ideas and visions.

6. Develop a keen sense to realize when a new product or service is needed. Envision that product in your mind. Answer these questions: What does it need to succeed? How can I produce and market it? How can I get others in the organization to "buy in"?

Communication

Your overall effectiveness as a leader is largely determined by your communication proficiency, one of the essential leadership skills. You may possess great visionary abilities, but if you cannot communicate clearly, people will not, and really cannot, "buy into" your vision for the future.

Great communicators are able to get people to follow them. Leaders such as Winston Churchill, Napoleon Bonepart, Mahatma Gandhi, and Lee Ioccoca were able to persuade people that their visions were accurate and their ideas sound.

Of course, for most of us our communication skill does not equal that of Churchill or Gandhi, but we must be able to inform others clearly and unambiguously. This can be learned.

Communication takes place through our senses, and it is enhanced when it's multi-sensory. Hearing and seeing is better than only seeing. Although communication is often dependent on only one of the senses, you should try to involve as many of the senses as possible: seeing, hearing, smelling, touching, and even tasting.

Appeal to as many senses as possible

According to textbooks, communication is divided into oral, written, and non-verbal (body

Notes

language). Although you may consider oral communication most important for a leader, the written word is often more powerful than the spoken word. People will accept "in print" information as true without taking the time or making the effort to verify it or to evaluate the source.

Some individuals find oral communication very easy and enjoy it immensely whether it's in the work place or in a social setting. Words seem to roll from their tongues effortlessly. Not only are the words well chosen and appropriate, but they also reflect logical thought. Do not be discouraged if your oral communication skill needs honing, for most of us are in this category. The important factor to remember is to take advantage of every opportunity to practice this skill, whether in a formal presentation or merely in a conversation with colleagues. Take the time to evaluate how well you are doing. Note when the communication seems to have gone poorly. To delve into the many possible reasons is beyond the scope of this book. However, you must be aware that the medium you use, your choice of words, your body language, the place, and the personality of the individual(s) involved may influence how your message is interpreted.

Being able to write well is important. We are all aware of the power of the written word. In fact, we refrain from putting something in writing out of fear it could come back to haunt us! Or we follow up a conversation with a written memo to ensure that there is no confusion. Again, take the time to review and assess your writing. Is it effective? If not, work on it.

When we consider the leader's communication skill, we usually think of the leader as the speaker, not as the listener. Remember that effective listening is two-way: Listening is an essential part of communication skill. (We devote a separate section to *Effective Listening*.)

Body language (frowns, folded arms, looking away, posture, etc.) is an important part of communication; it can either reinforce or detract from the spoken word. Because we are often unaware of our body language, it is difficult to correct or alter.

Finally, we need to recognize that there is no communication without understanding. Most of us have seen the communication model in one form or another (see page 18). In its simplest form, it consists of three boxes in a row. The first box is labeled Sender, the third box, Receiver, and the middle box, Understanding. Viewing the diagram you should expect that the receiver has a good grasp of the sender's message. The model

Notes

Be aware of your own body language

Notes

also stresses that communication is interactive or two-way, both the sender and the receiver are actively involved.

The significance of communication skill to leadership cannot be overstated, for understanding must occur before directed action can be taken. The realization of the vision is directly dependent on effective communication.

Leadership Tips

1. Keep people informed. It's better to error on the side of providing too much information rather than too little.

2. Before communicating and as often as possible, plan your thoughts mentally. Select words that efficiently convey your message. Plan the tone of the message you wish to impart.

3. Provide for opportunities within the communicating process to confirm that mutual understanding is occurring.

4. Be aware of audience reactions. Be particularly aware of individual's body language. It may indicate fatigue, a desire to ask a question or make a comment, or even excitement at your words!

5. Carefully listen. Hear all that is said, rather than only hearing what you want to hear.

6. Respond to comments to indicate that you understand.

7. Educate yourself about body language.

8. Ask for input—from followers, colleagues and friends—on the quality of both your written and oral communication.

9. Remember to use the *power of humor*. (Read the section in this book on humor.)

Notes

Listening Effectively

Effective listening is an ignored skill! Most people think of listening as merely a passive activity; someone else is doing the talking. Few of us think of listening as a skill, and even fewer have had any training in it. Most find it much more satisfying to be the talker, for usually it's the talker that gets the attention.

Listening is active, not passive

Listening is not passive; it requires concentration and involvement. It does not represent time for formulating your answer to whatever is being said. If it does, it means you are not really paying attention. Rather, you are planning your own talking.

Listening becomes increasingly important as you take on more responsibility and a leadership role. You should not begrudge the time spent in listening, because it pays huge dividends by building a trusting relationship and by promoting efficiencies.

There is a selflessness about effective listening. It is not judgmental. Its purpose is to achieve understanding, not to change the speaker. You may wish to change him/her, but this is not the time for it. First, you need to understand—to really listen to—the speaker.

Why is listening difficult? A major reason is that you think faster than a speaker can speak. You may have spare time in the listening situation, and this time can get you into trouble. Your mind wanders, first a little, and then, more and more until you lose touch with the ideas the speaker is conveying.

How do you prevent your mind from drifting? How do you listen well? The answer is by active participation in the situation, by asking yourself questions. You need to grasp the gist of the speaker's words: What are the underlying assumptions? What is the speaker's point of view? What is his/her body language communicating? What facts or factors support or do not support the message? In other words, you must make sure that your mind is involved in the listening situation. Also you should clue the speaker that you are listening by giving some active response: a verbal acknowledgment, eye contact, facial expression, or notetaking.

Effective listening also requires that you keep your emotions from coloring what you hear. Listening to ideas with which you agree is a pleasure, but listening to ideas with which you disagree is very difficult. Most people can hardly wait for the speaker to stop so that they can fire off a response. Unchecked, emotions act as filters

Notes

Emotions can be detrimental filters

Notes

allowing only your own "sanitized" ideas and point of view to enter.

Listening is a skill. It can be learned. You as leader not only need to be a good listener yourself but also to make sure your team understands the need for and develops listening skills. The goal of listening is understanding, a shared meaning, and you have a vested interest in making sure your team understands and shares the vision and goals of the organization.

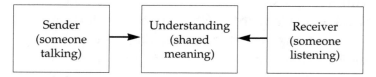

Listening is an integral part of the communication process. The traditional communication model for this process shows a message Sender and a message Receiver with the objective of Understanding or shared meaning usually placed between the two. This indicates that both the listener and the speaker have to make an effort at mutual understanding.

Leadership Tips

1. Practice active listening! Provide clues that you are actively involved: take notes, ask relevant questions, etc.

2. Concentrate. Try to empathize with the speaker.

3. Refrain from formulating an immediate response during your listening. Rather, concentrate on obtaining an accurate understanding of the speaker's words. Then allow the give-and-take to occur.

4. If possible prepare beforehand for listening: Think of possible outcomes and results, and of information that is needed. Consider possible negative outcomes.

5. Be prepared to accept revisions. Be aware of the common error of spending 90 seconds in expressing an opinion and 900 seconds in blindly defending it.

6. Be sure the physical environment is conducive to listening; check for good ventilation, a comfortable temperature, possible distractions, adequate lighting, background noise, etc.

Notes

Notes

Goal Setting/Establishing Priorities

Leadership involves the process of planning for the changes and achievements needed to realize the vision. New conditions, products, procedures, and practices are frequently required. Personnel changes are sometimes needed. During the planning process, it is usually necessary to make decisions and set goals about which future actions are required, and when the results are expected.

A goal is an objective to be met. It is the desired action or the result of an action. A plan is made to determine how and when to accomplish the goals. Duties or actions are assigned to persons to meet the established goals. Without goals at which to aim, very little is accomplished.

Because we cannot always accomplish all the goals at once, it is necessary to prioritize the order in which we will accomplish our goals. Which action to begin first, or which goals to accomplish first, may be influenced by many factors. The resources available in terms of money, people, time, space, and facilities will all have an impact on which goals can be met first. The success of the organization or project may depend on the ability of people to follow the order established for accomplishing the goals.

Notes

Managing all these priorities and assign-ments requires skillful leadership. The appropri-ate persons must be assigned to each phase of the project at the correct time. Acquiring the money, people, facilities, machines, and methods will determine the success of the project. The leader must communicate what has to be accomplished, the goals, the deadlines, and the important aspects of the project. After discussions and plan-ning with project members, it may be necessary to readjust the goals and priorities, and even the expected outcomes and results.

Many large projects that take time to accomplish require mid-course corrections. Periodic evaluations can pinpoint changes in the procedures that may be advisable. The people assigned to tasks may have to be changed. The keen observations of the leader can keep the pro-ject on course and on schedule.

Know that mid-course corrections are some-times necessary

Goal and priority setting requires intuitive thinking and a thorough analysis of all aspects and parameters: people, money, management, materials, machines, and methods. Skilled leaders are able to track progress and realign the goals and priorities as needed.

Notes

_____

_____

_____

_____

_____

_____

_____

_____

_____

_____

_____

Use "critical path'
analysis

_____

_____

_____

_____

_____

_____

_____

_____

_____

_____

Leadership Tips

1. When goal setting, include action plans, responsibility specifications, and the method for determining whether or not the goals have been attained. Specify acceptable tolerances.

2. Be sure goals are realistic and achievable.

3. Spend time and use your communication skills to get individuals to buy into the goal. Remember that this will usually not occur immediately.

4. Get into the habit of setting priorities in all areas, not just in those related to work.

5. Use "critical path" methods; that is, identify those activities that are critical in time and content to an overall activity. Failure in these activities holds up the entire project.

6. Set aside time each day to consider priorities. Make a list of desired goals; set the date and time to begin and finish each goal. Determine responsibilities.

Entrepreneurship/Risk Taking

Notes

An entrepreneur is a person who has the vision, motivation, perspective, problem-solving skills and commitment to take an idea and develop it into an acceptable product or service worth the effort and energies required to develop it.

To take your concept from a raw substance to a finished, sold product or service requires the ability to assess the future buying public's needs, as well as the ability to engineer the product development from its unrefined state to a finished product.

The entrepreneur risks his fortune and his reputation based on whether the product or service is correct, can be done, can be financed, and can be sold for a profit. If any of these conditions proves too difficult to solve, the product or service may never be perfected or accepted. It has to be the right product or service at the right time, for the right price, and marketed and often sold to a public that formerly did not know that it needed this product or service.

Most likely, the entrepreneur will have to convince people that his/her ideas are physically and financially sound. People may be asked to give monetary support before any product is

Notes

available. Real selling is needed to effectively communicate and convince people to accept the idea. Even after a product exists, it may take continued perseverance to develop its market.

An entrepreneur deserves to earn a profit that a product or service generates. The profits are payment for the many sleepless nights spent strategizing and worrying.

Leadership Tips

1. Be willing to begin small. Gain experience and expertise. Risk taking requires a reasoned, educated approach. Know the downside of the risk. Know the odds. Have a plan to deal with the downturns.

2. Know the answers yourself! Develop confidence by having thorough knowledge.

3. Determine what product or service is needed. Plan how to provide it at the least cost. Develop a marketing plan. Follow the financials to be sure that you are making a profit. Follow up with customers to make sure that the product or service continues to meet their needs. Get commitment for more purchases.

Motivation

In the opening pages we referred to the leader's need to energize followers—to create the sustaining desire to reach the goal. To do this, the leader must be able to show that the goal has value to the follower; the goal must have "appeal."

This desire or appeal is not necessarily something that will make the follower richer, more comfortable, or even happier. Many of us know people that strive and make great sacrifice to attain something for someone else's benefit. The goal nonetheless is something desired even if it's for another person, and in that it becomes valuable to them. The individual needs to know WIIFM (what's in it for me). The goal is something wanted.

The leader needs to recognize that motivating is an individual thing: What motivates one person may be a real turn-off for another. Thus the leader needs to get to know each follower in order to understand what will motivate him/her. To gain this understanding, the leader needs to invest time in listening to and interacting with each follower.

Understanding precedes motivating

Sometimes the leader is called upon to motivate a group without having the opportunity to get to know each person individually. Even then the leader must in some way "connect" with each person, perhaps through overall mutual agreement on an ultimate goal or through trust that was developed on an earlier project. Individuals may be willing to follow if they trust and respect the leader, and they recognize that their own goals and the leader's goals essentially agree. A congruency in goals is needed.

Whatever the source of desire to achieve the goal is, the goal must be worthy of the follower's effort to achieve it. The goal must have value, and often this value is not in terms of dollars. Each follower must be able to take ownership of the goal in some way; he/she must see not only the desirability of it but also his/her role in achieving it. This means that the leader understands each follower's strengths and weaknesses and, given these, can help identify a role that draws on the strengths.

Motivation must be sustained

Often we think of motivating as initiating or beginning an activity; that is, getting our followers or ourselves (self-motivating) to begin doing something. However, motivation means not only beginning an activity but also continuing or sustaining the momentum to finish it, for the end brings the desired goal that much closer.

Very basic to the leader's ability to motivate is the degree to which he/she has earned each follower's trust. The follower needs the assurance in his/her own mind that the leader's words and actions are congruent and that the leader's articulated vision and goals are correct and attainable.

In a way the leader becomes a salesperson when the desirability of the goal is not readily discernible to the followers. The leader then needs to help the followers understand why the goal is worth their effort, time and involvement, and how it will benefit them (WIIFM). Often this is the case when new and untried ventures are undertaken. In this case, the leader's ability to motivate becomes a real test of his/her skill and confidence.

Notes

Notes

_____

_____

_____

_____

_____

The individual's goals
and the organization's
goals must have some
congruency

_____

_____

_____

_____

_____

_____

_____

_____

_____

_____

_____

_____

_____

_____

Leadership Tips

1. Invest time in getting to know each follower. What are his/her concerns, personal goals, and particular interests? Determine each follower's "carrot," that outcome that he/she personally desires.

2. Always be ready to give praise and credit for a job well done. Remember there is no telling how far you can go if you give the other guy credit! Reward performance.

3. Invest time in discovering why an organizational goal should be desired by each follower. Be sure your followers understand goals and objectives.

Teambuilding

A leader realizes that he/she cannot run an organization alone. A group of managers is required to organize and manage the various groups of followers so that they work to fulfill the organization's vision. To keep the organization focused on meeting its goals, all members of the management team must understand what those goals are, know how to reach them, and see that the goals of individuals mesh with the organizational goals. Problems easily arise when managers don't agree on goals, priorities, or work plans. This situation causes divisiveness among managers and a feeling that managers are competing with each other.

Teambuilding is a skill that leaders must develop and continually exercise. The leader has to create an environment in which everyone can gain confidence through successful experiences working as a team member. The leader has to help the group set the goals and develop a work plan to accomplish them. Getting the team members to "buy into" the plan, feel a sense of ownership of it, and align their goals with those of the

Teambuilding is an on-going process

Notes

organization is a critical must. Each member has to see "what's in it for me" (WIIFM). Only then will team members align their goals with those of the organization and support each other. The resulting productivity and quality improvement that can be accomplished is astounding.

The best way to get team members to take ownership in the organization's vision, mission, and plan of action is to seek their help and input in developing each of these in a non-threatening atmosphere. It is logical to accept the plan of work when they helped formulate it. As the leader, you will find it much easier to get team members to follow your lead in accomplishing the objectives when they believe in the plan. In a hierarchical organization, the leader must first get the managers to believe and "walk the talk," so that they become an example for all team members. An environment that encourages risk taking and is non-threatening is one in which everyone wins. Then the benefits become "what's in it for us" (WIIFU)!

Leadership Tips

1. Remember that teambuilding rests heavily on your communication skill. Continue to work on honing this skill as you strive to bring together effective teams.

2. Formulate your own plans for the organization, but keep them to yourself initially. Ask for and then incorporate input from team members.

3. Work to eliminate causes of friction between interacting groups by encouraging and facilitating dialogue among them.

4. Reward successful groups; offer to help less effective groups.

5. Draw on your perspective (see page 44) of the organization to validate that the team objectives and goals are based on accurate data.

6. Be patient. Teams are not built overnight!

7. Play the E-game! (Next page)

Notes

Notes

E-game: A Teambuilding Exercise

Many activities and games are available for teambuilding. The E-game is one that we particularly like, because it not only requires team effort but also works on the team's vocabulary, one of the best predictors of success. (A more extensive vocabulary translates into a higher probability of success.) Of course, the activity should also be fun. Enjoy!

1. Divide a group of people into small teams of relatively equal size. (They can also divide themselves.)

2. Ask each team to identify a spokesperson.

3. Give the spokesperson a sheet of paper.

4. Instruct the teams to list as many words as they can think of that begin with the letter "e" and are related to leadership.

5. Set a time limit of 30 to 40 seconds.

6. At the end of the time limit, have each team present its list. The teams may challenge any word. The presenting team may rebut any challenge. Disagreements are settled by consensus or by vote of the participating teams.

7. If a word is successfully challenged, it must be eliminated, and the list for that presenting group is shortened.

8. The team with the longest list after all challenges have been resolved is the winner.

9. Continue with additional letters. Assign 10 points to a team with a winning list. The team with the most points wins.

Examples of E-words:

envision	emphatic
energize	efficacy
entice	economic
exert	effort
eager	embark
effective	enlighten
emancipate	enable
engage	emerge
efficiency	enervate
elate	earnest

Enjoy!

Notes

Encourage the teams to defend their words by giving situational examples

Notes

Commitment

It is not difficult for most of us to accept that we must be "committed" to an undertaking for it to succeed. Being committed squeezes out indifference, apathy and lukewarmness, and focuses attention, interest and action on the desired goal.

Staying focused is not always easy and can demand sacrifice. In fact, the word "commitment" implies an element of challenge; something is not easy about it. It also implies that you persist over time. Superhuman effort in short bursts is not uncommon. However, it is the sustaining effort that flows from being responsible that is outstanding.

Commitment implies a sustaining effort

Your ability to stay focused marks you as a leader. Commitment implies a tenacity, a holding on, a staying power. It is easy to talk about commitment, but quite a different thing to live it.

Commitment becomes an example to followers that applies across the Five Es of leadership. This skill enhances the envisioning, moves forward the engaging, enabling and energizing, and sustains the enacting. Each step in the leadership process demands your constant focus on the goal and the activities directed toward achieving that goal.

It is possible to be responsible for an unachievable goal. A relevant question is when does your commitment become foolish stubbornness. The answer rests in your ability to develop and use the leadership skills related to problem solving and decision making. If you have listened to counsel, examined the possibility of misinterpreting inflexibility as commitment, analyzed alternatives, and examined the decision-making process—you should be confident that your decision is based on solid reasoning. You have done your homework, listened to your heart and are comfortable with your decision.

Notes

Commitment is not stubbornness

Notes

_____
_____
_____
_____
_____
_____
_____
_____
_____
_____
_____
_____
_____
_____
_____
_____
_____
_____
_____
_____
_____
_____
_____
_____
_____
_____
_____

Leadership Tips

1. Choose your project(s) carefully based on intuition, research and discussions with other experts and peers. Be selective. Assume only the responsibilities with which you are comfortable and you find challenging.

2. Develop a "habit of commitment" once you are sure that you wish to commit yourself to an undertaking.

3. Be willing to review a commitment in light of new or changed information, but do not allow yourself to be easily diverted from your original course.

4. Take the role of devil's advocate as you reevaluate your commitment. Identify and respond to all reasons that you can think of for not being responsible for an undertaking.

5. Recall that by its very nature, commitment spans time. Identify associates that you feel have high levels of commitment and observe them over time. Observe how they resist efforts to alter the course to which they have pledged themselves.

6. Frequently articulate for followers how staying committed will achieve the desired goals. (Doing this requires communication skill.) Be a role model in this regard.

7. Be aware that your reputation is developed over time. Keeping commitments is a large part of establishing a highly regarded reputation.

Responsibility/Authority

As leader, you assume responsibility for the outcome of the team's work. Like it or not, you are responsible for whatever that outcome is. If it's success, you share the glory and learn from it. One wise saying states that there is no telling how far a person can go if he/she gives the other guy credit. In fact, you make sure that your team celebrates its successes. If failure is the outcome, you take responsibility and learn from it. This is a time that leadership can be particularly lonely!

Obviously, the team also needs to understand what went wrong, but you do not initiate learning by blaming and pointing fingers. Team members are not blind. Each member must deal with the failure. Blaming the team in general or one person in particular will only cause defensiveness and create an atmosphere that's anything but conducive to learning.

As you assume responsibility for the outcome, also assume you have the needed authority. In many instances, the leader does not have official authority, but through his/her leadership skills has the real authority. It is the wise leader, however, that emphasizes teambuilding and de-emphasizes his/her authority.

Accept responsibility, assume authority

Notes

An important part of being responsible is being able to delegate effectively. Often the likelihood of success is directly related to how well you can tap into the team's skills and abilities. This means that you understand the nature of the job to be done and that you know the skills and abilities of team members. Delegating responsibility effectively requires that you also delegate the needed authority.

It is the essence of leadership to be responsible for moving the team toward the goal. It is not possible to separate responsibility from leadership.

Leadership Tips

1. Practice taking on responsibility by volunteering. There are numerous worthy opportunities that can help you feel comfortable with having responsibility.

2. Be willing to take on additional responsibilities within your work group. However, be sure that you have adequate time to follow through.

3. Assume you have authority in line with your responsibility.

Initiative

Taking the initiative is the essence of leadership. Initiative means action, movement, or going forward. That is exactly what the leader does: He/She acts and is responsible for motivating (see *Motivation*, page 25) the followers to act.

Taking the initiative can be the catalyst that propels you into a leadership role. Because you have assumed the responsibility you become the person to contact. You almost automatically become the spokesperson for the undertaking. You gain the freedom to talk to people you may otherwise never have a chance to meet, and you may well have the opportunity to bring together a team that is willing to follow your lead.

Writers about leadership may use different terms, but their meanings are essentially the same. The leader is not passive; he/she is action-oriented, for leading is an on-going process. Stephen Covey in *The Seven Habits of Highly Effective People* identifies "being proactive" as Habit #1 of effective personal leadership. Peter Drucker opens Chapter 1 of *The Effective Executive* by stating that the effective executive is expected "to get the right things done," indicating the importance of action.

Notes

Remember that merely acting is not the point. The action must be preceded by decision making, that was preceded by problem solving, that was preceded by gaining an accurate perspective, that was preceded by listening and thinking. Taking the initiative flows from the vision as articulated by the leader. If you consider all of the leadership skills and traits discussed in this book, you'll note that the majority are in some way related to action that moves toward a goal.

Taking the initiative is closely linked to a willingness to take risks, for the final outcome is not certain. And of course risk taking implies the ability to deal with and learn from failure should it occur. The leader in a real sense "reaches into his/her toolbox of leadership skills and traits" and uses them to guide the action he/she sets in motion.

Notes

Leadership Tips

1. Volunteer, don't wait to be asked. Use your judgment, but be willing to take a chance.

2. Avoid procrastination. Even a small step can get momentum started. If the undertaking is large, divide it into parts that can be more easily comprehended and done.

3. Consider taking the initiative as gaining the freedom to network and to interact with people you might otherwise never have the opportunity to meet.

4. Realize that taking the initiative can be an opportunity to "learn by doing," or to develop leadership skills by taking on a leadership position.

5. Take the initiative: Clean up your own mess!

Section II

"The Toolbox" of Skills and Traits

Having these skills and traits helps
the leader be successful in a wide
range of situations and circumstances. He/She can draw upon
them as needed. We describe them
metaphorically as tools in a toolbox
that are available as needed.

Perspective

Why do you need perspective? Because before the vision statement, before the goals, before the strategies, before the tactics comes *perspective*—the understanding and knowledge of how things fit and of what should be and what is attainable.

Perspective is basic to judgment and is the source of inspiration that ultimately develops into a vision. The vision reflects your perspective. Decision making and goal setting also reflect your perspective that guides you in determining what the priorities should be and where you will get the best results.

You need perspective in terms of your internal organization. What resources can be tapped in terms of employee skills, equipment, and capital that mesh with the opportunities present externally? Where are the good fits? Where are the gaping holes that have no fits?

We suggest that gaining perspective can begin with this question: "Where are we bleeding the most?" Although this question immediately focuses on a problem area, it has the benefit of jolting us into reality; and, after all, perspective is worthless if it isn't based on accurate information about the "real" world.

In terms of people, you need to pay close attention to (1) what motivates individuals, (2) what their career goals are, and (3) how their personal goals and the organizational goals can be made to complement each other. Your perspective needs to incorporate an awareness of organizational politics: What power struggles exist? Where are automatic points of resistance to suggestions? How do the informal lines of communication connect? No doubt you can think of other important areas.

Gaining an accurate perspective does not just happen; it requires effort. Because perspective undergirds so much of the leader's vision, having accurate information is essential. We strongly suggest that you concentrate on developing your listening skills as well as keeping abreast of significant events in your industry or profession, and in the economy in general.

Gaining an accurate perspective demands time. It is a dynamic process, never complete, always on-going. To not make the effort is to fall behind. As leader, you must be able to chart the course without flip-flopping back and forth as new information surfaces. Your perspective clears away the smoke, so to speak, focuses attention, resources and effort, and gives direction.

Notes

Gaining perspective is a continuing process

Notes

Leadership Tips

1. Learn to analyze any situation relative to other facts and events.

2. Considering other events, rate the relative importance of one thing to another.

3. Realize that as events happen, the relative importance of an event may quickly change.

4. Help others keep their "buy-in" to the goals by keeping goals and their required action plans clearly in perspective.

5. Set up information gathering procedures that provide accurate data. Monitor these procedures to ensure their accuracy.

Fiscal Responsibility

We consider fiscal responsibility one of the "tool-box" skills that a leader can use to be effective. As the leader articulates a vision, he/she must sometimes gauge whether the vision is realistic in financial terms. It is one thing to dream, but the leader is not merely a dreamer. Awareness of the realities is essential in weighing alternatives and in setting courses of action that make sense.

When the leader has a good grasp of the financial realities, it inspires a higher degree of trust in his/her leadership. Followers can take comfort that it is unlikely that money crises are going to surface suddenly. Followers can also take comfort that the leader cannot be bamboozled or deceived by a "number thrower."

Depending on the leadership situation, the leader should understand such financial items as the balance sheet, income statement, cash flow, return on investment measures and budgets, and the budgeting process. The leader should make it his/her business to have a clear understanding of whatever financial information is relevant to the functioning of his/her group. This understanding can be helpful, for example, in shortening a list of alternatives by allowing the immediate elimination of those that are not fiscally sound.

Notes

Fiscal responsibility is not a straightjacket

Fiscal responsibility should not be viewed as a straightjacket that hems in creative thinking and action. Rather, it should be considered a starting point that encourages thinking of new and more effective methods. An organization's resources are always limited, and often as the saying goes "necessity is the mother of invention." Fiscal responsibility can be the necessity that leads to innovation.

There is some controversy about whether fiscal information should be shared with followers. We suggest that, used correctly, fiscal information can be a motivator. The leader needs to make sure that this information is presented in an understandable fashion and that followers can see how their actions can positively affect the "bottom line," the overall profitability.

Some people feel that numbers are boring, confusing, and even misleading. The leader cannot afford to be bored or confused by numbers, and the success of his/her group could well depend on his/her not being mislead by numbers presented in a way to obfuscate. In fact, the leader's ability to use numbers to clarify and explain can enhance the trust that followers have in the leader.

Leadership Tips

1. Mentally know what financials are involved with a project:
   - What will it cost?
   - Where will the money come from?
   - What can be done to minimize production costs?
   - What percentage of the costs will be attributed to material, labor, overhead, selling, financing, and distribution?
   - What should be the expected profit?
   - What is the payback to investors?

2. Study the basics of accounting; "know the numbers!"

Notes

Enthusiasm

Have you ever really noted when you are enthusiastic? If you do, you'll discover something you probably already intuitively know: You're enthusiastic when you are doing or are planning on doing something that interests you, something that you really want to do. That's not earthshaking, but too often we fail to realize how infectious or magnetic our enthusiasm is. It's as if other people want to get in on a good thing. Enthusiasm engages people!

Enthusiasm engages people

Your enthusiasm also becomes a motivator, an energizer. You, the leader, are the head cheerleader for the team. Can you imagine a cheerleader without enthusiasm?

Too often and too easily work becomes drudgery. Day-to-day pressures obscure the vision and goals. Your enthusiasm inspires people to get beyond the immediate concerns that must be dealt with, done, and delivered.

Your big question, of course, is how do I as leader become and stay enthusiastic? You are human and, as most people, you do not operate at a fever pitch day in and day out. Fortunately, enthusiasm does not mean intensely excited activity. Enthusiasm does mean an expressed positive attitude towards the goals and objectives. It means looking for the points to celebrate while recognizing that there is room for improvement.

As with most good things, enthusiasm is not an accident. It requires effort; it requires wanting to be enthusiastic! Enthusiasm is often fueled by a willingness to take on challenges. The leader must see the threats as opportunities, not in a foolhardy sense but with recognition that there is no victory without risk.

An important fact for you to recognize is that enthusiasm usually—although certainly not always—requires that you are in generally good health (see the section on *Self-Renewal*). Treating your health as a priority has ramifications in many areas of leadership, and having enthusiasm is one of these areas.

Leadership Tips

1. Focus on the positive. Use positive imagery. Be aware of the negative but don't let it dominate your thoughts.

2. Network with positive people. Enthusiasm is infectious!

3. Keep smiling!

Notes

Notes

Attitude

"He has a real attitude!" You may have used or heard this expression. In today's usage, we know it means the person has some type of mindset that is difficult for others to deal with or understand. It's definitely not a compliment. It clearly points out that our attitudes affect how others see us and how they react to us.

We often refer to attitudes as being positive or negative. If a person's mindset or attitude is usually upbeat and happy, we describe it as positive; if it is usually dour and faultfinding, we term it negative.

Attitudes are easily transferred; some call them contagious. This means a negative attitude in a work group can eventually "infect" others, causing low morale and productivity losses. Thus the leader's attitude as well as followers' attitudes is very important. No one wants to or enjoys associating with a person who is consistently negative.

The important point to remember is that *attitudes can be changed*. We control our attitude. Many of the situations we confront are beyond our immediate control, but the attitude or mindset we draw upon in reacting to the situations is

Attitudes can be changed

very much within our control. We're not doomed to some inborn attitude; we can change.

Zig Zigler, in his book, *See You at the Top,* refers to a Harvard University study that revealed "85% of the reasons for success. . . were because of our attitudes and only 15% because of our technical expertise. . . ." Attitudes are very important; you cannot afford to ignore attitudes.

As the leader, take stock of your own attitude. Are you generally upbeat and positive in your approach to people and situations? Or do you find yourself frequently complaining and faultfinding? If you are prone to being negative, begin now to make a conscious effort to stop complaining and to look for the positive aspects of people and situations.

Also pay attention to the prevailing attitudes of followers. A negative attitude can be an automatic way of responding, and breaking a habit or helping others to do so is not easy. You may find that the negative attitudes of only one or two individuals have infected the entire group. Or morale is low for some reason, making it much easier for everyone's attitude to turn negative.

The first step is to make sure that your own attitude is generally positive and that it can

Notes

Notes

serve as an example. Then begin what may be a long and difficult process to turn around others' negative attitudes. You will draw upon many leadership skills, especially your commitment, patience, persistence, and communication skill. Negative attitudes often result from feelings of being "out of the loop" when changes occur. Make sure that you have listened to individuals, sought their input, answered their questions, tried to show how each person has a significant role to play and that you have articulated the vision as clearly as possible. You will find that some individuals need more of your time than others, but be careful not to ignore any person. Even those who have generally positive attitudes need to be kept informed.

Leadership Tips

1. Become aware of your own attitude. Is it generally positive? Resolve to maintain an optimistic attitude by emphasizing the positive.

2. Think positively. Look for the upbeat side. Your attitude should mirror what you would like to see in other individuals.

3. Invest time in learning about attitude formation and change. This may involve reading or taking classes in areas related to psychology.

4. Read *Your Attitude Is Showing* by Elwood Chapman. Make the book available to others.

Observation/Perception

As the leader, you must be able to observe and evaluate the conditions and factors of the environment to assess when things are going well and when they are not. You must be able to determine when people are happy, when they do not comprehend directions, or when they do not understand what is expected of them. You need to be able to sense if customers desire something other than that which they say they want, or if customers are not satisfied.

The skill of being observant and perceptive to visual clues, activities, results, interactions of people, business numbers, and human emotions can be learned. It takes concentrated effort to focus on clue-giving events. You must build time into your schedule for observing and listening. You must interact often with your customers and associates to observe behavior and to listen to their comments. You must be able to assess the consequences of your actions and their actions.

Look for clue-giving events

Careful observation and astute listening must be practiced. A leader uses all of his/her senses to "read" situations for clues. Interactions with persons should be verified so that you know that what is said is not only heard but understood. When listening, you may want to restate

Notes

what a person is telling you to be sure that you understand the person's full meaning. That action also reinforces to the other person that you are listening and comprehending.

As you observe, you also need to interpret what is observed in perspective with other events. You must try to determine how persons are feeling when they speak. If you expect to motivate people, you have to know what excites them into action and what kills their enthusiasm. People say they want to be treated the same when, in reality, each person wants something different. To know how to deal with each individual, you must read "the signs."

To achieve productivity, you as leader may need some help, guidance, and training. People who can provide support are available.

To be a successful leader, you must be a good listener and observer. A leader sometimes seems to have a crystal ball. The reality is that the leader has worked diligently to develop his/her ability to perceive and keenly observe.

Leadership Tips

1. Assume a questioning attitude. Look for clue-giving events, such as high turnover, absenteeism or increased customer complaints. Distinguish between symptoms and causes.

2. Know that actions really speak louder than words. Pay attention to how individuals are spending their time.

3. Dig into financial data. Don't be put off by numbers. Try to see the "big picture."

4. Do the exercise below.

Observation in Action

The leader needs to be a keen observer. Developing this skill takes time and effort. We feel that this short exercise drives home the point.

Look at the large triangle below and quickly identify the total number of triangles. How many do you see? We say there are nineteen!

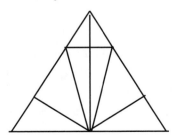

Notes

Problem Solving

Leaders must be good problem solvers. Leaders are recognized for their ability to assess a situation, determine what is wrong, investigate the causes of the problem, and engineer the solution with vision and insight. This kind of skill can often turn an organization around.

The first step in the problem-solving process is to define the problem accurately. This is not as easy as it sounds. Often when a problem is identified, it turns out to be only a symptom of a much larger problem. Upon investigation, a series of glitches may unfold that have always been part of a less-than-perfect process.

The second step in the problem-solving process is to break the problem down into its simplest parts to look for the actual causes. It is these causes that must be removed to correct the situation. When performing the problem-solving steps, brainstorm for causes and answers to the problem with the involved individuals. They usually have many ideas about the causes. Look for agreement on the cause(s). The group may wish to use some of the helpful problem-solving techniques such as flowcharting, check sheets, and cause-and-effect diagrams. (Read *How to Implement Total Quality Management* by Miles and Donna Southworth.)

The third step is to determine the solution. Again, seek the consensus of the group as to what the best solution is. If a consensus is not possible, at least get a compromise.

The fourth step is to implement the solution. To see if a solution works, try it on a small scale. Do not change the process until the new method is tested. If it proves correct, then implement it in full. But be warned, changing an entire production or service procedure without trying it out first can lead to chaos and no solution!

Problem-solving skills are not something with which people are born. The leader as a critical observer of the entire process should be able to direct people to find the root cause of an inconsistent product or service, and eliminate it. A change in a process may be all that is needed. A more drastic solution may require reengineering to completely change a product or service.

You may want to seek an outside opinion from a person who has experienced resolving similar dilemmas. After evaluating the entire situation, this person can suggest "quick fixes" and/or long-term corrections, or verify that your approach is correct. A leader usually is skilled at problem solving but may not have the process knowledge or the time to focus on the problem.

Notes

First test a solution on a small scale

Notes

Seeking an outside opinion can be a sign of smart leadership.

Develop your problem-solving skills. Surround yourself with good problem solvers. Their input enhances everyone's efforts. They are worth their weight in fifty dollar bills!

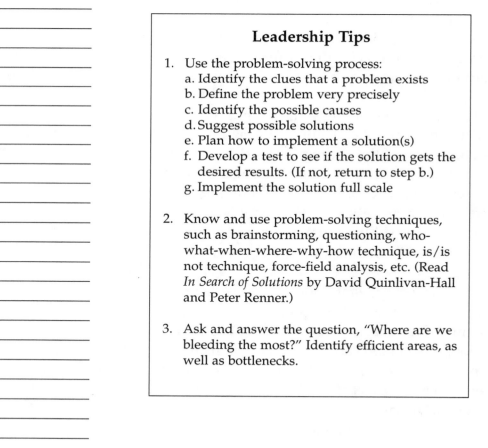

Leadership Tips

1. Use the problem-solving process:
    a. Identify the clues that a problem exists
    b. Define the problem very precisely
    c. Identify the possible causes
    d. Suggest possible solutions
    e. Plan how to implement a solution(s)
    f. Develop a test to see if the solution gets the desired results. (If not, return to step b.)
    g. Implement the solution full scale

2. Know and use problem-solving techniques, such as brainstorming, questioning, who-what-when-where-why-how technique, is/is not technique, force-field analysis, etc. (Read *In Search of Solutions* by David Quinlivan-Hall and Peter Renner.)

3. Ask and answer the question, "Where are we bleeding the most?" Identify efficient areas, as well as bottlenecks.

Networking

One of a leader's most valuable tools is his/her ability to network with other people. Every field has experts and gurus who are known for their extensive knowledge about a particular topic or skill. Your key to success may be the fact that you know experts or someone who does and can refer you to them.

A rule of thumb is that you should be able to solve any problem with only three phone calls —and that means anywhere in the world. If you cannot do this, you do not know the right people. It is a sign that you are not meeting the people who can help you.

Develop acquaintances and friendships with people who have similar professional interests as yours. Be active in professional groups that are structured around your profession. Join social associations whose members have similar interests to yours. Meet with technical, and research and development people from other companies. They might be in a position to answer questions for you in the future.

Join and be active in professional groups

Participate in management groups centered around the kinds of skills needed in your area. Don't just go to meetings; get involved.

Notes

Volunteer to serve on committees and boards. The committee meetings are where you really get to know people. Remember too that it is often in the social setting that you hear important technical information or learn about key persons you might want to talk with later.

Networking will often help you find the key people you need. Obviously, it could help you personally should you decide to change jobs, remembering that in today's business climate that could be an unplanned change.

Networking is a valuable skill; the benefits are often mutually rewarding.

Leadership Tips

1. Join organizations related to your work and be active in an area that interests you.

2. Make a point of knowing other persons in your field.

3. Socialize with experts or leaders in related and unrelated fields.

4. Volunteer to work on professional or local committees to help others who might learn from you.

5. Remember that being known is good publicity for your organization and for you.

Competence

If you were to check the dictionary definition of the word "competence," you would discover that this word has an underlying meaning of "being adequate" or "sufficient" for the task at hand. Being competent means having skills and traits that are adequate.

We don't subscribe to this definition when it's applied to leadership. In this book, competence means more than merely being "adequate." It means doing the job so well that followers recognize you as a source of inspiration, help, and guidance.

Competence involves being technically and "people" knowledgeable. Technical competence, usually the easier of the two to achieve, can be gained by study, reading, hands-on work, observing "how it's done," etc. A technically competent person is able to do the job in a more-than-adequate manner. Competence implies that time is not wasted by misfire starts and stops, or by trial and error. Rather, there is direction in the approach and the completion of the job.

"People" competence means the ability to relate to people in such a way that, given your technical competence, co-workers are willing to be followers! In a sense, people competence is not something unique in itself. It is the result of being a good communicator, a good listener, a good motivator, and a good teambuilder. Having developed the skills and traits of leadership has earned you the trust of your followers.

Because "people" competence means dealing with the feelings and perceptions of others, it is not as clearcut as technical competence. The leader must be able to deal with different personalities and different attitudes; the leader deals with greater uncertainty and more subjectivity here than in the area of technical competence. This does not mean that technical competence is easy to attain, but it does mean that the leader will probably expend greater effort in developing competency in dealing with people than in developing technical competency.

Required technical competencies change very quickly

A leader needs to be critically aware that needed competencies change very quickly, particularly technical competencies: What is new today is "old hat" tomorrow. Obviously then the leader needs to take the initiative to maintain his/her competency. This is particularly important in gaining the perspective (see page 44) needed to set the vision for the organization.

If followers do not perceive you as competent, they will probably not accept your leadership. A competent leader gives the followers comfort that he/she knows "the ropes" and cannot be easily mislead or bamboozled. Work hard to be competent. Then work hard to be sure followers perceive you as competent!

Leadership Tips

1. Know your field technically. Read about it enthusiastically.

2. Hone your people skills. Read, attend seminars, observe, and learn from others.

3. Take inventory by completing the Personal Leadership Assessment at the end of this book. This assessment should help you pinpoint your strengths and weaknesses.

_____
_____
_____
_____
_____
_____

_____
_____
_____
_____
_____
_____

_____
_____
_____
_____
_____
_____

_____
_____
_____
_____

Confidence and Poise

Confidence and poise are closely related: Poise flows from having a nice measure of self-esteem and confidence in yourself. Confidence flows from your faith and commitment to the vision. Often this confidence becomes the inspiration to followers, engaging and energizing them.

Your self trust and self assurance rest on faith in your own judgment. However, being human you make mistakes. Therefore, your confidence needs to be based on having listened carefully to followers and colleagues, and on having analyzed the situation and facts. Having done your homework, you need to project steadfast belief in the course of action that you have selected.

Being confident does not mean you have the answer to every question; no one can be expected to know everything. Nor does the same degree of confidence transfer to every situation. It falls to the leader, however, to project confidence, keeping in mind that risk and uncertainty are ever-present realities.

Being confident makes having poise that much easier. Besides meaning a self-confident demeanor, poise is the ability to feel comfortable in any situation and with all people. Poise enables you to say or do the appropriate thing; it helps you "to think on your feet." It helps you understand the impact on others of your words and actions.

Both confidence and poise are skills that can be learned with effort, patience, and practice. Both confidence and poise require your understanding of all relevant parameters of a project, whether they are technological, psychological, social, etc. You must have accurate information on which to base your judgments. Poise means not only appearing confident but also being confident. Sometimes this combination of confidence and poise is referred to as a "presence"or having charisma. Whatever terms are used, confidence and poise are important leadership skills.

Notes

Notes

_____
_____
_____
_____
_____
_____
_____
_____
_____
_____
_____
_____
_____
_____
_____
_____
_____
_____
_____
_____
_____
_____
_____
_____

Leadership Tips

1. Start small. Build on successes. A succession of successes reinforces confidence.

2. Do your homework. Be prepared. Confidence and poise come much more easily if you are thoroughly prepared and can respond smoothly to opposing viewpoints.

3. Realize that you will never have perfect knowledge and that you cannot be expected to have all the answers. Work to identify the level of risk and uncertainty that you feel can be prudently tolerated.

4. Be truthful with others and with yourself. Trying to mislead or lying may have short-term benefits, but it will destroy your self-esteem and whittle away at your confidence and poise.

5. Pay attention to details that could detract from your confidence and poise. Dress appropriately, know the social graces, become aware of customs or established traditions within the group. Although these are not the essence of confidence and poise, paying attention to them can only be advantageous.

Patience and Persistence

Notes

Patience and persistence are leadership skills although we may hesitate to identify them as such immediately. After all, isn't the leader supposed to see that things get done, not to sit around waiting for something to happen? And if the leadership process is effective, should persistence really be needed? Shouldn't the leader have identified the desirability of the goal? Shouldn't the followers be making haste to attain it?

In the real world, as we are all painfully aware, things do not always progress as expected. Leadership requires a degree of patience and persistence, both of which take effort. If you were to check the dictionary meanings, you would find that both patience and persistence involve some type of straining: Patience involves restraining from an action so that another individual "has a chance." Persistence involves straining to go forward in spite of obstacles.

Patience gives a follower a chance "to do." Perhaps a new employee needs time to gain perspective or a "seasoned" employee needs time to develop a new expertise. Having patience reflects confidence in your followers that they will ultimately perform. It takes sound judgment to decide when to exercise patience. When will

Notes

Persistence is based on reasoned judgment

allowing a little more time result in vastly improved output? When will giving an individual a second chance result in a fiercely dedicated employee? When will listening a little longer result in much greater understanding? You do not want to be perceived as weak and indecisive, but having patience is a legitimate action.

You also need to judge when persistence is needed. Persistence arises from your vision of the future, for the vision will never become a reality without hard work. Responsibility falls to you, the leader, not to give up, but to inspire and motivate others to continue to see the desirability of the goal—to persevere.

Although the dictionary uses the word "stubborn" in defining persistence, the leader cannot afford to be stubborn; leading is not an ego trip. Persistence is based on your reasoned judgment that the goal continues to be desirable and ultimately attainable. If circumstances change, the goal may also have to be changed or at least altered along with the plan to attain it. Persistence does not mean inflexibility or an unwillingness to change; it does mean an unwillingness to change easily. Persistence requires your continuing analysis and commitment even in the face of obstacles that would cause the fainthearted to give up. Your persistence becomes an inspiration to others and continues to engage them in striving for the goal. Persistence can be a real test of your leadership skills.

Notes

Leadership Tips

1. Cultivate your listening skill. Effective listening requires patience. As you work to develop patience, you synergistically develop your listening skill and vice versa!

2. Analyze in terms of the long term and the short term. Having the long-term goal in mind helps you have the patience that may be required to attain the ultimate goal.

3. Make it a habit to refuse to give up any undertaking easily. Persevere.

4. Make it a point to observe and to read about people whose persistence or patience is noteworthy. These observations or accounts can serve as inspiration and models for developing these skills.

Notes

Time is a most precious resource

Time Management

Effective use of time is a characteristic of a leader. Being able to accomplish most of the important tasks and yet reserve time for business colleagues, as well as for personal and family pleasures, is a skill that must be learned and practiced.

Each person has a given amount of time. What will distinguish you from others is how you assign and prioritize what you do with that time. A leader will have many requests for his/her attention. Prioritize those tasks you think are the most important. Assign blocks of uninterrupted time to accomplish those important tasks. Try to prevent interruptions of those time blocks. Reserve some time for yourself and your family. Plan time for others to meet with you. Prevent others from setting your schedule for the use of your time to accomplish their agenda and not yours. A great deal of diplomacy is required to deny people from accessing your time whenever they demand it. An open-door policy is not always the best policy for all hours of the day. Other people have to realize that you have your own prioritized schedule.

Accept the fact that you will not be able to do everything you would like to do. Make a list of all those things or tasks that, if not done, don't make any difference in your life, job or career. They probably don't need to be done, or perhaps they can be delegated to another person. *Effective delegation* is a leadership skill and often a necessity in your time management effort.

Leadership Tips

1. Consider your time a most precious resource:
   - Prioritize the most important tasks
   - Schedule your time to complete those tasks
   - Minimize interruptions of blocks of time
   - Eliminate unnecessary uses of your time
   - Delegate tasks to others when appropriate
   - Don't try to do everything
   - Respect other people's time

2. Make use of small "bits" of time. Put reading or writing material where you can easily reach for it when traveling or waiting. Use waiting time effectively.

Notes

Dealing with Frustration and Emotions

Leaders are frequently confronted with the need to deal with frustration and emotions, either in themselves or in others. Frustration is something that thwarts or disappoints and, in most cases, is seen as a detriment or unwanted occurrence. Often frustration leads to some type of emotional reaction that is likely to be counterproductive.

We must acknowledge, however, that many emotions are positive and productive, such as joy and enthusiasm. The leader does not really have to "deal with" these, for they usually enhance productivity and the environment. It is the emotions that have negative consequences, such as uncontrolled anger and outbursts of invectives, that the leader must develop skills to control. Negative emotions often arise from frustrations or from disagreements, and if left unchecked can cloud judgment and lead to irrational behavior.

Key in dealing with frustration and emotions is recognizing them and being aware of their continuing presence—in yourself or in others. The skills needed to handle emotionally-charged situations fit squarely under the topic of people competence (see pages 63-65), for as you develop skills in recognizing and dealing with

frustration and emotions, your people competence improves.

Emotions have several characteristics of
which you need to be aware. (Recall that we are
considering emotions that have or could have
negative consequences.) They range in kind,
intensity and duration. They can be irrational,
and they often have physical manifestations (red
face, or increased heartbeat).

Because each person's emotional makeup
is unique, learning to deal with emotions can
seem a daunting task, especially when you consider that you must also deal with your own
emotions as you seek to deal effectively with
those of other individuals. Of course, there is no
template that fits all cases; however, there are
strategies and techniques that prove helpful.

The first step is to know the person (this
includes yourself). What are his/her concerns,
goals, aspirations, and "hot buttons" (things that
the person feels strongly about)? Recall that motivation also requires that you know these. Pushing
a hot button, or thwarting a goal can easily set off
the emotions and a consequent reaction.
Knowledge of a person's emotional makeup
comes through communication: talking with the
person, discussing his/her objectives, listening to

Notes

Notes

Work to avert head-on confrontations

his/her plans, and sharing information in general. Then, if you see some event approaching that would upset the person, you can take action to avert head-on confrontation about it. Normally this means talking with the person. It may be effective to open the discussion by verbalizing the person's concerns yourself, thereby letting him/her know that you understand. The person is sure to add comments as you proceed.

As the discussion continues, you will be able to judge whether the person is able to proceed rationally. If not, you may want to ask the person's forbearance, and schedule another session, giving the person a chance to sort out his/her feelings and return to rationality. Dealing with frustration and emotions does not mean you avoid confrontation at all costs; it does mean that you try your best to make sure that the other person has a chance to voice his/her position and that he/she knows you have listened and have heard it. Keeping communication lines open and flowing is essential.

If a person does "blow," how should you deal with it? Realize that some people have loud and angry outbursts, while others seethe in silence. The age-old technique of simply encouraging the person to verbalize his/her feelings and by "listening out" the individual continues to be effective. Eventually the person winds down, perhaps from sheer exhaustion. Then you should indicate that you are very aware of how he/she feels. Throughout these discussions, you should try to identify the problem, for often a person avoids stating the real reason(s) for being upset. Gradually approach the most sensitive topic(s), recognizing that you may have to test the waters and retreat several times before determining that the person is ready to discuss the topic calmly and rationally.

Be aware that changing the environment may help communication. Suggesting that you both take a walk or retreat to a private area while you talk may have a calming effect on the person in that he/she has your undivided attention.

A person's emotional makeup affects his/her attitude. Most individuals enjoy working with upbeat people—those who have positive attitudes. A negative emotional outburst within a group can have a demoralizing effect; people want "it" to just go away. They want to get on with the tasks at hand and not spend their energies worrying about how a sensitive person is going to react to something. Thus in dealing effectively with frustration and emotions, the leader helps to ensure that the group as a whole has a positive attitude.

Notes

Notes

Culture impacts emotions

It is also important to recognize that cultural differences affect emotional response. Some cultures react to situations very vocally and loudly, while others are much more reserved. Of course, the outward manifestation is not an accurate indicator of the depth of the emotion. In today's diverse work arena, you must be an especially keen observer and an astute listener to deal effectively with frustration and emotions.

This area will require constant attention throughout your career, for in dealing with frustration and emotion, you are not dealing with black and white. Rather you are in the gray area, and after all, life usually takes place in the gray area! In today's work place, it is also important to be aware of the danger to yourself and to others if an individual becomes truly distraught and/or violent. Intense emotions often lead to violence. This means you must take reasonable measures at the very least to ensure safety. These measures may include physically restraining a violent person, prohibiting his/her access to an area, or calling security. Know your company policy as it relates to this disruptive behavior, and know the avenues of help that are available to you.

Leadership Tips

1. Know the "hot buttons"—both yours and the other person's. Become aware of the circumstances that are sensitive or troublesome, and develop methods for calming people.

2. Develop a repertoire for dealing with negative emotions:
    *   Take a walk or suggest taking a walk with someone who needs to regain his/her composure.
    *   Retreat to a private area to take a breather or suggest a private place to talk with someone who is upset.
    *   Talk with a trusted colleague.
    *   Expand your knowledge in this area. Read, attend seminars or workshops where you learn about effective "people techniques."
    *   Try seeing the situation from the upset person's viewpoint. If only in your mind, role play the "she/he says, I reply" situation.

3. Talk with other individuals about this topic when it is not an issue. Know what help is provided by an Employee Assistance Program. Keep Cool!

Notes

Notes

Dealing with Stress and Fatigue

We know that we live in a fast-paced, demanding world. More must be done with fewer people, decreased resources, and less capital. Competitors are intense; technology changes daily. Change is the constant!

These pressures place increasing demands on all individuals. Not only must the leader deal with his/her own stress and fatigue levels but must also recognize that others are experiencing similar pressures.

Stress is rooted in external causes, frequently related to people relationships—a difficult employee, a fault-finding colleague, or an explosive boss. Stress can occur when the level of expertise demanded is near the limit of the individual's "comfort zone."

Each person reacts to stress in a unique way. Some people become irritable, some grow quiet and withdrawn, some talk or eat compulsively, some chain smoke, some become extremely nervous, and the list continues.

Because the leader's role is to focus on the goal, he/she must deal with stress in a way that does not interfere with reaching the goal.

Dealing with stress requires that we recognize what is stressful to us. It is important to sort out, as well as we are able, exactly what it is that causes us to be anxious, for then we can begin to deal with it. We need to recognize that we don't have to allow ourselves to become "stressed out." Pressure filled situations will continue to occur, but we do not have to allow ourselves to become "victims" of the situations.

Analyze what is stressful, and then look for strategies to neutralize its effect. If a person causes us fretfulness, perhaps we need to interact with that person more often to establish trust. If we are worried because we have far too much to do, we need to learn to say "No." We cannot be all things to all people. We need to select the areas in which we want to participate, spend time and expend energy. Setting priorities is key to composure!

As in dealing with frustration, a vigorous workout, a long walk, or some relaxing activity is helpful. However, stress is best dealt with by determining and eliminating its causes.

The usual way that we handle increased demands is to stretch out the work day, often extending it late into the night. The result is a chronic feeling of fatigue. Not only does fatigue

Notes

Learn to say "No" tactfully

Notes

cause our thinking to be fuzzy, but it also can be very dangerous if either mental or physical alertness is required.

Being organized greatly alleviates stress levels. If we are organized, we can demonstrate to ourselves as well as to others why we should not undertake additional commitments.

Know that stress levels and fatigue are not likely to improve until you address the problem(s) and work on solutions. Be proactive and selective in your undertakings.

Leadership Tips

1. Prepare well for situations that you consider stressful. Don't proscrastinate. Be proactive.

2. Be organized. Be able to demonstrate your current commitments. Keep a calendar.

3. Learn to say "no" tactfully. Don't assume you have superhuman stamina.

Learning from Failure

Notes

Who wants to learn from failure? No one wants to "take credit" for a project that was unsuccessful. Maybe it is not pleasant to learn from failure, but because you're human, sooner or later you will have this opportunity!

You need to realize that learning from a mistake or error is just that—an opportunity. To ignore this moment would be a missed opportunity. You probably feel at least some embarrassment, and you would like the entire situation to disappear. This reaction is normal and very understandable, but you need to realize that there is increasing recognition that people who have experienced failure and have "gotten beyond it" have the resiliency and self-esteem needed to succeed in today's work place.

Failures are erasable

How do you learn from a project gone awry? You do so by stepping back and analyzing what went wrong. Doing this, we know, is much easier said than done, for often a seemingly obvious answer is not the entire answer. The failure most likely resulted from an interplay of factors, some of which were not obvious, otherwise they would have been addressed. The objective of this analysis is to identify the possible causes. The ultimate objective is to prevent a recurrence.

Notes

_____
_____
_____
_____
_____
_____
_____
_____
_____
_____
_____
_____
_____
_____
_____
_____
_____
_____
_____
_____
_____
_____
_____
_____
_____
_____
_____

Leadership Tips

1. Be aware of the BIG clue: If you are making the same mistakes, you have not learned from failure. Don't make the same mistake twice!

2. Don't be afraid to try: "Nothing ventured, nothing gained." Current successes quite easily blot out past failures.

3. Recall that you may be judged as lacking in initiative if you are afraid to try new ventures and take risks.

Heart/Human Relations

To some, human relations means "touch-feely stuff." Human relations is not easily quantified and, therefore, not worthy of much concern. Some think human relations is merely common sense, obeying the Golden Rule, or simply "being nice." These views severely understate the scope and importance of effective human relations skill.

Human relations is more than observing the Golden Rule

This skill has a broad perspective; it encompasses many other skills, including motivating, teaching, mentoring, coaching, training, counseling, mediating, understanding, empowering, disciplining, listening, empathizing, teambuilding, and the list goes on. Human relations skill is the leader's ability to engage, enable, and energize individuals so that they enact what is required to achieve the goal(s).

If asked, most people would probably rate themselves high in human relations. They would offer that they are nice to their co-workers, that they genuinely like other people, that they greet others politely, that they give others a chance to talk, that they give credit to others when it's due, that they say thank you when appropriate, and many other good responses. All of these assertions are probably true, and all of these activities are part of human relations, but there is more . . . .

Notes

Human relations is the skill to develop and maintain relationships that positively impact morale and productivity. Human relations is more than just getting along with people. It is the skill to relate to individuals so that organizational goals are enhanced.

Communication skill (see page 11) plays an essential role in human relations. Good relationships are built on foundations of fair, honest, and frequent two-way communication.

The work environment repeatedly presents difficult situations that require effective human relations skill. Think of the young, energetic, and capable employee who feels entitled to a promotion even though no position is currently open. Do you. . . Ask him/her to be patient? Make a new position? Increase his/her salary? Offer a new challenge in the current position? Ignore the situation? Suggest that he/she look elsewhere for a new position? In another case, think of the person who is not working up to his/her potential. How do you. . . Approach and motivate this underachiever? Sustain the motivation?

People problems outnumber technical or process problems, and as your responsibility increases, human relations skill becomes more important because your accomplishments depend largely on the work and efforts of others. Thus, from a selfish point of view, human relations skill helps you to look good. From an ethical point of view, you want to exercise good judgment and fairness; human relations skill makes doing this easier and less stressful.

You need to take action to develop this skill that is really a set of skills. An effective technique is to identify people who are proficient in human relations and observe them. Perhaps you can adopt or adapt some of their methods. Asking for input from trusted colleagues may give insight to areas that need attention. Role playing, watching videos, and reading about the topic should all prove helpful in developing human relations skill. Working on improving your communication skill will have a spillover effect on improving your human relations skill.

Along with human relations skill, we suggest that you work on developing a trait that we call "heart." It is the ability to temper decisions with genuine concern about the impact of those decisions on others. This does not mean that you refrain from making hard decisions, but it does mean that you do your best to look for win/win solutions in terms of individuals and the organization. "Heart" says that you not only seek what is best for the organization, but that you also seek

Notes

Your success may depend on the success of your followers

Notes

what is best for individuals. In today's work place we are often made painfully aware that the once unwritten contract (if you do your job well, you have a job) between an organization and its employees has all but disappeared. Individuals feel little loyalty to an organization that fires people after years of productive work. A leader seeks to strengthen the loyalty rather than destroy it, and he/she does this by seeking solutions that are win/win rather than win/lose.

It is good to remember that in dealing with people there is always give and take. Sometimes the individual gives more than is required and sometimes the organization does. This relationship in itself is a win/win situation, for each will rise to the occasion as needed. "Heart" says that the leader values this relationship and will do whatever is in his/her power to strengthen it.

Leadership Tips

1. Work on strengthening your communication and listening skills, and your human relations skill will improve automatically. Adopt human relations techniques that you observe to be successful.

2. Ask for input from trusted colleagues on how they think you could improve in this area.

3. Develop the trait called "heart" by always first identifying and working toward win/win solutions in terms of the organization and individuals.

4. Take advantage of reputable workshops that seek to develop your human relations skill through discussion and role playing.

5. Educate yourself about the legal issues in the human relations area, particularly with regard to the laws on sexual harassment.

Notes

Notes

Self-Renewal

The word "burn-out" can represent varying meanings and varying degrees. Comments such as, "I dread going to work," "My job's not fun anymore," and "I don't see any future in my job," may signal the onset of burn-out, when there is little excitement or looking-forward to a day. Self-renewal is the antidote to burn-out!

Too often self-renewal is viewed as a luxury, something you "do" when times are good and operations are going smoothly. It's seen as a "reward" for achieving an objective or meeting a target or goal.

This is a mistaken notion!

Self-renewal is a responsibility. Its essence is not just a costly vacation at an exotic seaside villa, nor is it a trek into the wilds of the north country. It is simply a time set aside to recharge, reconsider, and recommit. With day-to-day demands, it is extremely easy to lose a clear focus on goals—both personal and organizational. Self-renewal is the opportunity to refocus.

Self-renewal requires you to separate yourself from the daily demands. It rightfully allows for relaxation and recharging the mental and physical self. It includes a rethinking of personal goals, organizational goals, and the "fit" of the two. It allows you to take inventory of "where you are," "where you want to be," and "where you've been effective and where not."

In a sense, self-renewal is personal quality control in action. Self-renewal gets you back into the "control area." It allows you to analyze variances, and it helps you to gain the perspective (see page 44) needed for a leadership role. Self-renewal provides time to think, to sort out, to analyze, to evaluate, and to plan.

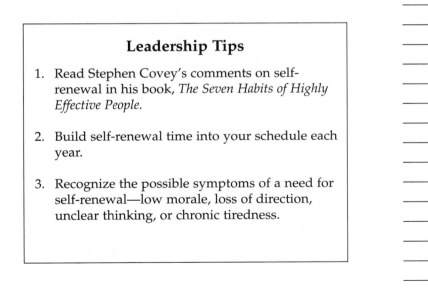

Leadership Tips

1. Read Stephen Covey's comments on self-renewal in his book, *The Seven Habits of Highly Effective People.*

2. Build self-renewal time into your schedule each year.

3. Recognize the possible symptoms of a need for self-renewal—low morale, loss of direction, unclear thinking, or chronic tiredness.

Notes

Self-Esteem

Underlying and giving vitality to what a leader does is his/her self-esteem or positive impression of self. Leading requires the ability to envision a goal and to energize others to strive for it. To do this, the leader needs to be free of excessive self doubts about his/her ability. In a sense, self-esteem is the bedrock of leading. With it the leader "knows thyself," is at ease with himself/herself, and does not squander time and effort trying to assume some fake persona.

Having self-esteem does not mean "being smug" or "self-righteous"—quite the contrary. The person with self-esteem strives to improve but realizes that this is the challenge of humankind. To improve is fun and exhilarating; it's constant "fresh air"! The current self is the stepping stone to something better and is, therefore, highly prized and valued.

Self-esteem, like many leadership traits, is essentially an interior thing; the individual develops it. Even amid put-downs and criticism from others, the person with self-esteem is able to put these comments in perspective, to realize that some criticism is well-founded and deserves attention, and some should be ignored.

Often a person with low self-esteem is a braggart, especially one who while bragging tries to tear others down. Certainly a person can take pride in his/her accomplishments and talk of them. However, to dwell on them excessively and repeatedly, and to point out the failings of others in the process indicates an inability to measure up to the self's expectations. A constant need to pare others down so that the self looks better indicates a real lack of self-esteem.

In bringing together a team, the leader should pay attention to self-esteem. Studies show that high self-esteem translates to high productivity. Again, it's as if self-esteem is the fresh air that energizes and frees people to try new things, to take risks, and to do!

Notes

Self-esteem directly relates to productivity

Leadership Tips

1. Consider your own self-esteem. Know that shortcomings are not failings engraved in stone. Rather, they are opportunities to improve.

2. Take note of how often you speak negatively of others. Avoid doing this.

3. Seek out people with high self-esteem. They get things done!

4. Celebrate self. If you don't believe in yourself and your ability to reach goals, why should anyone else believe in you?

Honesty, Integrity, Morality

Practicing honesty, integrity, and morality builds trust

People develop within themselves a sense of what is right or wrong. That sense can vary depending on your country of origin, your religious upbringing, and your family values. An honest and moral person will not try to take advantage of another person. An honest and moral person will always try to treat other people in a fair and equitable manner.

Mother Teresa was once asked for her advice on how to live a good life. She said, "Pray a lot. Never do anything you know is wrong." That pretty well sums up how a good person should live his/her life. An honest and moral person will do what is right even when nobody is watching. Treating everyone truthfully and not cheating anyone are the first steps to building other people's trust in you.

We can identify leaders throughout history who started out to be great leaders but who exhibited few moral values or honesty. While they were identified as leaders for a time, they eventually were brought down. Their grand plans for a perfect world in their own minds came to ruin. We don't subscribe to a leadership devoid of moral values, honesty, or integrity.

Dishonest leaders are eventually toppled by the very people they try to lead.

Leaders with integrity are known as persons who always can be relied upon to do what they say. They will follow through with action plans. They can be counted on for assistance when needed by a colleague or friend. They will stand up for what is right and will try to prevent actions that are not honest and fair.

From an organizational viewpoint, it makes good sense to practice honesty, integrity, and morality. Employees that value these qualities tend to gravitate to organizations that also value them. These same employees tend to be highly productive.

Develop and practice an unquestionable sense of truthfulness and fairness in everything you do. You will never regret it. These character traits will serve you well throughout your entire lifetime. You will be trusted and respected. Employees, stockholders, business leaders, and family members will respect you for these traits. They will back you when you ask for their support, because they know you can be trusted.

Notes

Notes

_____
_____
_____
_____
_____
_____
_____
_____
_____
_____
_____
_____
_____
_____
_____
_____
_____
_____
_____
_____
_____

Leadership Tips

1. Know that trust is fundamental to leadership. Mutual trust is developed by. . .
   - always telling the truth
   - treating all persons fairly
   - keeping commitments and finishing projects
   - refraining from backbiting
   - never cheating another person or company
   - praising others whenever possible
   - helping others whenever possible
   - respecting family values.

2. Read about people who are identified as being honest and moral.

3. Have a religious belief and advisor.

Leader's Prayer.

To think without confusion, clearly.

To act from honest motives, purely.

To trust in God in heaven, sincerely.

Humor

Humor has come into is own! Frequently classi-
fied as a "sixth sense," humor is a valuable leadership skill. There is increasing recognition that
humor can have a very positive effect when used
appropriately. It is the spice that helps to main-
tian an enjoyable atmosphere. We even refer to
the power of humor. It can relieve tension, set
people at ease, help establish camaraderie in a
group, serve as an icebreaker, and heal damaged
relationships. There is increasing awareness that
humor positively affects a person's physical well
being. We wager that a hearty laugh each day can
make your life more pleasurable!

*Recognize the power
of humor*

Humor takes many forms: a humorous
story, pun, overstatement, understatement, satire,
or irony. Most of us have fond memories of company roasts in which all of the above forms of
humor were used. Culture often plays a part in
humor. Usually there is some kernal of truth,
often implied, that makes humor effective.

Humor can also be dangerous! In the work
place it should never single out religious or ethnic groups as targets. Not only might such use be
demoralizing to an individual or group, but it
could also be identifed as harassment. In such a
case, the effect of humor would be exactly the

Notes

opposite of what it should be. The "when in doubt, don't" rule should be strictly followed.

The person who can tell an appropriate joke or a good story is always appreciated, even needed. You should work to develop this skill so that you can use it when the situation calls for some tension relief, attention getting, etc. Making yourself the object of a joke or story can be very effective, for in doing so you let people know that you can laugh at yourself. You have enough self-esteem that you are not threatened by being the subject of a hearty laugh.

Leadership Tips

1. Accumulate a set of humorous stories and one liners that you can tell well and that are appropriate for many different occasions. You should practice using humor whenever the opportunity presents itself.

2. Encourage the use of appropriate humor; laugh at others' appropriate jokes. Humor can add significantly to a group's cohesiveness.

3. Exercise caution with the use of ethnic language; avoid sexist jokes.

4. Be willing to be the brunt of another's tasteful humor. Willingly laugh at yourself.

Section III

Approaches to Leadership Styles

Leadership Styles

Whenever leadership is considered, eventually the topic comes around to leadership style, that distinctive or characteristic manner or method of acting for the accomplishment of a goal. The traditional approach is to identify several different styles, such as authoritarian, permissive/laissez-faire, and democratic. The interesting and important fact to remember is that the leader's style is not "stuck" in any one of these categories. Partitioning leadership merely provides a convenient method for discussing a complex topic. Also, it is true that a person may be inclined towards a particular approach, but our observations indicate that the leader develops a range of styles that he/she can draw upon as needed by various situations.

This range can extend from the authoritarian style at one end of the leadership spectrum to permissive at the other end. Traditionally, we describe the *authoritarian style*, also called autocratic or dictatorial style, as a "do it the way I tell you to do it" decree method with little or no input from the follower. Carried to its ultimate, authoritarian leadership almost requires the follower to take on a robotic nature; he/she reacts as the leader dictates. We know that this would be an extreme, and yet we can think of situations

Notes

Develop a range of leadership styles

that demand immediate and focused attention for which this style would be appropriate. It is true that some people are inclined to use an authoritarian style more often than other techniques.

At the other extreme is a *laissez-faire style*, meaning that the leader has an almost "hands-off" approach. He/She lets the followers "do their thing" when and how they want to. (You may question whether this is leadership.) Certainly organizational goals are at risk with this method.

Between these two extremes—authoritarian and laissez-faire—is *democratic leadership style* that gives direction and freedom, but not too much. Usually, this approach is held out as the ideal leadership style.

The democratic method represents the traditional approach to leadership. We suggest a few additional styles, intending that the labels point to a leader's distinctive manner: *persuasive, inspiring, charismatic,* and *participative.*

Leaders with the *persuasive style* use what we term a sales approach. They know what they want and set out to convince others to fall in line with them. Some compromise along the way may be necessary, but by using their well-developed persuasive skills, they manage to get agreement and movement towards the goal.

The *inspiring leader* appeals to the followers' emotions and intellect. Others are attracted by something they admire in the leader: It might be the leader's exemplary life of service to others, his/her ability to uplift spirits, or his/her cunning to present challenges that excite followers.

The *charismatic leader* has that "certain something" that automatically attracts followers. Charisma is not one characteristic but a set of attributes that evokes approval from others.

The *participative style* is essentially like the democratic style. The leader has struck that desired balance between not too much control and not too much lack of control. He/She seeks the involvement of followers in problem solving and decision making. Although this leadership style can take years to develop, followers often thrive in the atmosphere it creates.

If you examine your type of leadership, you could probably pinpoint your dominant style on the leadership spectrum. However, leadership style is not static. You should seek to develop a range of styles so that you are able to change your approach as the situation warrants.

Notes

Range of Leadership Styles

Spectrum of Styles	Leaders What are their dominant styles?

Authoritarian/Dictatorial
  Commanding
  Unbending
  Militant
  Forceful
  Self-confident
Persuasive
  Convincing
  Flexible
  Cajoling
  Compromising
Inspiring
  Challenging
  Uplifting
  Fulfilling
Charismatic
  Enveloping
  Intriguing
Participative/Democratic
  Consensus-building
  Teambuilding
Laissez-faire
  Non-directing
	Hannibal
	Caesar
	Pharaoh
	Bonaparte
	DeGaulle
	Elizabeth I
	Hitler
	Lenin
	Grant
	Patton
	MacArthur
	Jesus
	Moses
	Ghandi
	Churchill
	Truman
	Martin Luther King
	Mother Teresa
	Lincoln
	Franklin
	Reagan
	Powell

Figure 3: Although leaders employ a range of styles, they usually gravitate toward a particular style, a distinctive manner of acting for the accomplishment of a goal.

Section IV

Leadership Self-Assessment

Notes

Personal Leadership Assessment

Try this self-assessment now, before you read the book and as you begin concentrating on developing leadership skills and traits. Then, read the book, work on the skills and traits, and retake the assessment in three months. A higher score should indicate that you are improving your leadership skills and traits. The objective is to assess your own strengths and weaknesses so that you can work on self-improvement.

"To thine own self be true."

Evaluate each question on the following scale:

Poor	Fair	Average	Good	Excellent	Not Yet Applicable
1	2	3	4	5	0

Vision

1. Have I articulated a vision?   1 2 3 4 5 0

2. Is the vision clearly publicized?   1 2 3 4 5 0

3. Do I regularly refer to the vision?   1 2 3 4 5 0

4. Did I seek input in formulating
   the vision?   1 2 3 4 5 0

5. Have I recently revisited the vision? 1 2 3 4 5 0

6. Do followers understand the
   vision-setting process?   1 2 3 4 5 0

Communication

Notes

7. Do others listen carefully when
   I speak?   1   2   3   4   5   0

8. Am I pleased with my writing?   1   2   3   4   5   0

9. Am I able to "think on my feet"?   1   2   3   4   5   0

10. Do I know my own body language?   1   2   3   4   5   0

11. Am I aware of others' body language? 1   2   3   4   5   0

12. Do I seek to minimize a confronta-
    tional atmosphere?   1   2   3   4   5   0

13. Do I try to use all five senses?   1   2   3   4   5   0

14. Do I help followers improve their
    communication skills?   1   2   3   4   5   0

Listening

15. Am I an active listener?   1   2   3   4   5   0

16. Do I concentrate on the speaker's
    words?   1   2   3   4   5   0

17. Do I prepare for listening?   1   2   3   4   5   0

18. Do I help followers develop listening
    skills?   1   2   3   4   5   0

Goal Setting

19. Do I set goals—long and short term? 1   2   3   4   5   0

20. Do I prioritize goals?   1   2   3   4   5   0

21. Do I set aside time each day to review
    goals and priorities?   1   2   3   4   5   0

Notes

22. Do I encourage followers to set goals? 1   2   3   4   5   0

Entrepreneurship/Risk Taking
23. Am I willing to do my homework to minimize risk?   1   2   3   4   5   0

24. Once prepared, am I willing to go forward without inordinate delaying? 1   2   3   4   5   0

25. Do I attempt to assist followers to approach risk taking sensibly?   1   2   3   4   5   0

Motivation
26. Do I consider motivation an important part of my responsibility?   1   2   3   4   5   0

27. Do I try to determine what motivates each follower?   1   2   3   4   5   0

28. Do I attempt to find win/win solutions so that personal and organizational goals mesh?   1   2   3   4   5   0

29. Do I reward performance?   1   2   3   4   5   0

30. Do I give credit when it's due?   1   2   3   4   5   0

31. Do I refrain from correcting in public? 1   2   3   4   5   0

Teambuilding
32. Do I seek WIIFU (what's in it for us) while recognizing that each team member needs to know WIIFM (what's in it for me)?   1   2   3   4   5   0

33. Do I seek to establish a non-threatening atmosphere that welcomes new ideas?   1   2   3   4   5   0

34. Am I vigilant for points of friction
    that may be developing?   1 2 3 4 5 0

35. Do I encourage followers to develop
    teambuilding skills?   1 2 3 4 5 0

Commitment

36. Am I selective in committing my time? 1 2 3 4 5 0

37. Do I consider a commitment almost as
    a sacred trust?   1 2 3 4 5 0

38. Do I follow through on what I say
    I will do?   1 2 3 4 5 0

39. Do I let my followers know that I value
    commitment?   1 2 3 4 5 0

Responsibility/Authority

40. Am I willing to be responsible for the
    outcomes of my leadership?   1 2 3 4 5 0

41. Do I delegate effectively?   1 2 3 4 5 0

42. Do I encourage celebrating successes
    of followers?   1 2 3 4 5 0

Initiative

43. Do I avoid procrastination?   1 2 3 4 5 0

44. Do I consider taking action as a means
    of gaining freedom or access that I might
    not otherwise have?   1 2 3 4 5 0

45. Do I encourage followers to try new
    things and to take the initiative?   1 2 3 4 5 0

Notes

Notes

Perspective

46. Have I set up information-gathering processes—both upstream and downstream?   1   2   3   4   5   0

47. Am I able to answer the question: "Where are we bleeding the most?"   1   2   3   4   5   0

48. Do I share information so that followers can also develop an accurate perspective?   1   2   3   4   5   0

Fiscal Responsibility

49. Do I have a good grasp of financial information?   1   2   3   4   5   0

50. Do I share financial information in a way that's appropriate for followers' use?   1   2   3   4   5   0

51. Do I encourage followers to develop an understanding of financial data?   1   2   3   4   5   0

Enthusiasm

52. Do I make a special effort to be enthusiastic?   1   2   3   4   5   0

53. Do I maintain my physical health so that being enthusiastic is that much easier?   1   2   3   4   5   0

54. Do I let my followers know that I value their enthusiasm?   1   2   3   4   5   0

Attitude

55. Am I usually upbeat and positive?   1   2   3   4   5   0

56. Do I try to convey to followers that
    positive attitudes are valued?   1   2   3   4   5   0

Notes

57. Do I make communication with followers
    a top priority, thus enhancing the
    atmosphere for positive attitudes?   1   2   3   4   5   0

Observation/Perception

58. Do I look for clue-giving events or factors
    (low morale, high turnover, increased
    customer complaints, etc.)?   1   2   3   4   5   0

59. Do I pay attention to how employees
    are spending their time?   1   2   3   4   5   0

Problem Solving

60. Do I use the problem-solving process?   1   2   3   4   5   0

61. Am I aware of different problem-
    solving techniques?   1   2   3   4   5   0

62. Do I encourage followers to become
    problem solvers?   1   2   3   4   5   0

Networking

63. Do I make networking a priority?   1   2   3   4   5   0

64. Do I encourage my followers to
    network?   1   2   3   4   5   0

Competence

65. Do I vigorously stay abreast of the
    technology in my field?   1   2   3   4   5   0

66. Do I continue to improve my
    people skills?   1   2   3   4   5   0

Notes

67. Do I encourage followers to develop both their technical and people skills?   1   2   3   4   5   0

Confidence and Poise

68. Do I prepare well?   1   2   3   4   5   0

69. Do I educate myself about the social graces?   1   2   3   4   5   0

70. Do I help followers develop self-confidence and poise?   1   2   3   4   5   0

Patience and Persistence

71. Am I willing to see the long-run implications and sacrifice immediate gains for better long-term returns?   1   2   3   4   5   0

72. Am I willing to give people a second chance, realizing that most individuals want to do a good job?   1   2   3   4   5   0

73. Am I an example to followers in being patient and persistent?   1   2   3   4   5   0

Time Management

74. Do I act with the realization that time is a precious resource?   1   2   3   4   5   0

75. Am I always prepared to make use of even small "bits" of time?   1   2   3   4   5   0

76. Do I help followers develop time management skills?   1   2   3   4   5   0

Dealing with Frustration and Emotions

77. Am I aware of my own and my followers' hot buttons (sensitive topics)?   1   2   3   4   5   0

78. Do I have a set of techniques for dealing
with negative emotions?   1 2 3 4 5 0

79. Do I encourage followers to develop
skills to deal effectively with frustration
and emotions?   1 2 3 4 5 0

Dealing with Stress and Fatigue
80. Do I prepare well, thus eliminating
a powerful stress factor?   1 2 3 4 5 0

81. Do I keep a calendar so that I am always
aware of commitments and can easily
demonstrate that my "plate is full"? 1 2 3 4 5 0

82. Am I able to say "no" tactfully? 1 2 3 4 5 0

Learning from Failure
83. Am I able to subordinate the fear of
failure to a willingness to take
reasonable risks?   1 2 3 4 5 0

84. Am I willing to allow my followers to
learn from failure?   1 2 3 4 5 0

Heart/Human Relations
85. Do I continue to try to improve my
human relations skills?   1 2 3 4 5 0

86. Do I always first seek win/win
outcomes?   1 2 3 4 5 0

87. Do I have sufficient knowledge of laws
related to human relations?   1 2 3 4 5 0

Self-Renewal
88. Do I regularly seek opportunities
for self-renewal?   1 2 3 4 5 0

Notes

Notes

_____
_____
_____
_____
_____
_____
_____
_____
_____
_____
_____
_____
_____
_____
_____
_____
_____
_____
_____
_____
_____
_____
_____
_____

89. Do I consider self-renewal an on-going necessity?   1 2 3 4 5 0

90. Do I provide my followers with opportunities for self-renewal?   1 2 3 4 5 0

Self-Esteem

91. Am I aware of the level of my own self-esteem?   1 2 3 4 5 0

92. Have I observed in myself or in my followers that positive self-esteem leads to greater productivity?   1 2 3 4 5 0

93. Do I zero in on self-esteem as a quality that I value in myself and look for in team members?   1 2 3 4 5 0

Honesty, Integrity, Morality

94. Am I always truthful?   1 2 3 4 5 0

95. Do I follow the Golden Rule? ("Do unto others as you would have them do unto you.")   1 2 3 4 5 0

96. Do I give the "benefit of the doubt"?   1 2 3 4 5 0

97. Do followers trust me?   1 2 3 4 5 0

Humor

98. Do I value humor as a leadership skill?   1 2 3 4 5 0

99. Do I encourage the use of appropriate humor in the work place?   1 2 3 4 5 0

100. Am I willing to laugh at myself?   1 2 3 4 5 0

Notes

Tracking Progress

Date

Score _____   _____

Score _____   _____

Score _____   _____

Score _____   _____

Score _____   _____

Score _____   _____

Section V

Reminders. . .

Notes

Reminders. . .

The following comments, recommendations, and advice should help you develop some additional skills and social graces as you perfect your leadership ability.

Loyalty is expected of both leaders and followers. No work place and few situations are perfect. Remind yourself of the plus factors of your position and your work environment. Make constructive suggestions at the right time and place, but *never* badmouth your employer or firm, especially to people outside of the organization. *If you must be critical, discuss the situation with a trusted colleague who will keep your confidence.*

As a leader, one of your most valuable skills is to build confidence for your policies and procedures so that employees trust you and are loyal. Loyalty becomes a reality when leaders treat individuals honestly and fairly.

Working with younger people. . . Respect them for their knowledge and don't talk down to them just because you have more experience. Realize, though, that they may not know an important historical connection or procedure. Find a way to ask if they need any background information without sounding as if you are challenging their knowledge or lack of experience. Offering information without asking may annoy them if they already know the facts or details.

Working with older people. . . Avoid the temptation to stereotype the older person as difficult to get along with or unwilling to change. Our advice is to avoid jumping to conclusions and to practice the three Rs: be Respectful, Responsible, and Reliable. Respect the older person's knowledge and experience. Be willing to ask his/her help or advice when it's appropriate. Be willing to assume additional responsibilities that you can confidently handle, and be very sure to keep your commitments—be reliable.

Other people's values may not agree with yours. Be aware that their values may influence their decisions and dealings with you. You don't need to share a person's values to work with them or do business with them. Avoid arguing about the differences; simply discuss them if they come up. It is okay to have significant differences of opinion and yet to get along.

Cultural differences often influence the way a person thinks, acts, talks, meets people, and arranges business transactions. Respect the differences; recognize they exist and don't do or say anything that would insult the person or his/her background. It is okay to discuss the differences

Notes

in a non-threatening manner; simply be respectful of people's cultures.

Walk the talk! Building trust and confidence is done by *always* doing what you say you will do. It could take years for you to overcome one mistake. Your integrity means that you can be trusted to do what you say. Even one lie or failure to do what you say can hurt your credibility and ability to lead. Everyone will probably hear about it. Don't try to cover it up. Admit it and move on to prove that you can be trusted to keep your word.

Admit mistakes. Trying to cover up mistakes or blaming someone else will only lead to mistrust. Try to make amends to anyone who suffered from your mistake, even if it is only a sincere apology.

Help individuals maintain self-esteem. People like to be respected, especially by their peers. In this day of constant change, make sure that the lack of knowledge by an individual does not cause him/her to lose the respect of peers. Provide opportunities for education. Keep people informed about the latest policies and procedures so that they don't lose face with colleagues.

Be visible to followers. People want to know that you know who they are and what they do.

Get around your organization for no other reason than to talk with individuals and show that you care about their concerns and suggestions. They need to feel wanted and valued. They want to know that they can talk with leaders and management and be heard. They will respect you for doing this.

Be visible to superiors. Your career depends on your being known by your supervisors, upper managers, and your peers. Get around where you can bump elbows with upper managers. Lunch where they lunch. Volunteer to work in organizations to which they donate their time. Join the same club if possible. Volunteer to take on projects that will make your talents visible. You won't regret it.

Dress for success. Dress appropriately. That says it all! We know that first impressions are important, and no matter how much we may not like it, our attire speaks loudly. Dressing appropriately gets the issue out of the way so that you can spend "mind time" on more important matters.

Today it is common for business people to travel in jeans with a sweater or blazer. A blue blazer, khaki or gray slacks/skirt are acceptable in business meetings and social functions for men and women except when a dark blue suit is required.

Notes

Notes

In many organizations, Fridays are casual days, when less formal business attire is acceptable. Abide by the Friday dress code: Usually jeans are not acceptable, and shirts with collars are required. Don't "push" the code, seeing how much you can get away with! Again, dress appropriately and be free to put this issue aside.

Greeting acquaintances. . . When greeting someone you have met before, walk up to the person and say your name, thus putting the person at ease. It is often difficult to recall a person's name when meeting him/her away from the place you normally meet. NEVER walk up to a person and say, "You don't remember me, do you?" This puts the person in an embarrassing position as you have challenged his/her memory. You want to make a good impression, not a bad one.

Shaking hands with someone is often the time you create your first impression. Shake hands with a dry, firm grip. You should not have a limp, damp handshake. When a woman offers her hand, shake it gently but firmly.

Introducing people. . . Always introduce people when a group forms. Don't expect people to introduce themselves unless you have forgotten their names and decide it is less of a *faux pas* to not introduce them than to admit you forgot their names. As a conversation starter, give their names and tidbits about their connection with you. Praise or good words about them are also good conversation starters and win friends.

Name badge. . . Wear your name badge on your right lapel or in the center of your chest. This ensures that your name badge is readable by the person you are meeting while you shake hands. A badge worn on the left lapel or pocket is difficult to read.

Grapevine. . . Use the grapevine to your advantage. Every organization has an informal communication network that can spread information faster than memos or e-mail. Learn how to use it in a positive method. Be observant. Who in the organization delights in being the first to know information and likes to spread that information. It is always a good thing to make sure that this person knows the accurate facts, otherwise you will spend a good deal of time correcting for misinformation in the grapevine.

Identify troublemakers. Every organization often has a few people who delight in causing trouble, usually in a misguided attempt to gain the admiration of their colleagues. Identify these individuals so that you can involve them in a positive way. With reinforcement, they can often be

Notes

contributors rather than detriments to progress. Other individuals will be appreciative of your success in working with these people.

Table manners. . . The lack of knowledge about table manners can cause anxiety and make you feel ill at ease when you really want to make a good impression. Therefore, take the initiative now: Read about etiquette, observe those "in the know," and practice the rules of etiquette, making them your *standard operating procedures* in all areas.

Avoid sexual harassment accusations. Know the law on this issue and abide by it religiously. Protect yourself by *willingly* attending required workshops. Treat the topic seriously. Work to get rid of any behavior that could be construed as sexual harassment. Set the example. Make it clear that there is no choice on this issue.

Professional terminology. . . Develop a good vocabulary. Doing so is indeed an obtainable leadership skill. If you gradually acquire a list of pre-thought out words that define and describe your objectives and the reasons for them, you will be comfortable when called upon to explain and communicate actions that advance your goals. This is part of the **enabling** process. When you have done your homework, you will never find yourself lost for words.

Also, words we use reveal a great deal about us independent of the meaning they convey. Referring to women as the "weaker sex" or to a new employee as a "greenhorn" or to an older person as a "codger" says something about how we think of these individuals. Avoid using such terms and words in the the work place, but more importantly examine why you would want to use these words in the first place.

Be aware of expressions that can be demeaning to others. Saying to someone, "you don't understand" or "you've got it all wrong" can easily be an affront. Use expressions that don't get in the way by offending others. Say, rather, "let me explain how I see it," thus setting the stage for a give-and-take discussion attuned to idea sharing and problem solving.

Rewarding and recognizing individuals for doing a good job is a leader's job! Don't neglect this responsibility, for in relationships the "little things" are big things. A positive comment, a complimentary memo, an acknowledgment— whatever the form—are not only the right things to do but can be powerful motivators. Individuals often go beyond the call of duty. Develop the habit of looking for these occurrences, so that you can "catch" the person and recognize his/her contribution.

Notes

Notes

Groupthink is never good. It sets in when you prevent opposing or divergent ideas from having a fair hearing. Put in place procedures that prevent groupthink. When implementing change, purposely seek out the broadest range of ideas. Work to keep an open mind. If you sense that groupthink is setting in, appoint or ask for a volunteer to be a "devil's advocate" whose serious purpose is always to present the other side(s).

Idea incubation may be needed in some instances. You may sense from people's reactions that they need time to think about an idea that's been presented. The thought needs time to gel; the individuals need time to "kick it around" in their minds. Don't harp. Give people time to accept a new idea or concept.

Letting go of an idea or venture can take courage and decisiveness. As the song says, "you've gotta know when to hold'em, know when to fold'em, and know when to walk away." There is no clear rule to follow here. As a leader, you are walking that fine line between perseverance and foolhardy stubbornness. Of course, you can be guided by financial information, trend information, advice from colleagues, and even intuition. However, the decision to "walk away" can be one of the most difficult you'll ever make.

Thank you. . . The magic words! Said sincerely, these two words go beyond merely acknowledging input or help from others; they point to that for which money does not compensate. When you use thank you, mean it. In this day of frequent international travel, we suggest learning these two words in as many languages as you can. Said sincerely, "thank you" expresses heartfelt appreciation that enhances relationships.

Gateway people are those who maintain and even control the schedules of others. Be sensitive to the concerns of these individuals; they are charged with screening out individuals and events that are time wasters or unwanted interruptions. That may sound harsh, but that's their job. High-handedness on your part only enhances their screening skills! Be courteous and be patient; "pleasant persistence" will usually get that appointment you want.

Name facility is a strange expression, but by it we mean the ability to recall names accurately. This can be an important leadership skill. We have all had the unhappy experience of being introduced to persons and almost instantly forgetting their names. Recognize the problem and prepare for it. Make it a habit to concentrate during introductions. If this is a particular problem, try some of the techniques experts suggest, such

Notes

as associating the person's name with something that will jog your memory. Our experience is that *concentration* is the key.

Speed reading is becoming increasingly important in this age of information overload. Studies show that speed readers usually retain more of the information they read than do read "plodders." During the speed reading learning process, comprehension falls initially but then quickly picks up and accelerates. Learning speed reading requires a time investment, but it is an investment that pays constant dividends. Also, being able to speed read earns the admiration of others!

Working with people of different religions. . . Always give the other person his/her space. Most would agree that religion should not be a factor in the work place; religion is a private matter. Religious beliefs are deeply held. Getting along in the work place does not mean that you must set aside deeply-held doctrine. It does mean that you respect others' religious philosophies even though you may not accept them as your own. You should expect the same respect in return.

Sometimes it's appropriate and even helpful to discuss religious beliefs. If the other person is able to talk about religion without becoming heated or accusative, such a discussion at an appropriate time can be enlightening. In general, never belittle another's religion. With any controversial topic, avoid discussing it in the work place, because the result can be the loss of productive time.

Working with people of different political beliefs. . . Observe the same cautions that relate to religious beliefs. Political beliefs are usually deeply held and often are not based on rational thinking. Sometimes they reflect family traditions. Therefore, it's best to choose less volatile topics. If the conversation gradually turns to politics, avoid flagrant statements that could trigger another person's flashpoint. Listen politely and steer the conversation to a safer topic.

Habits . . . Be very aware of the ones you have developed or are developing. These "prevailing dispositions" can be good or bad. As we all know, they are reinforced through practice and, therefore, become increasingly ingrained. Always being late, smoking, and talking incessantly are a few examples of "bad" habits; their opposites are "good" habits.

    The important point to know and remember is that we can control our habits; we are not victims of an outside force causing our habits. We may need some help. However, bad habits

Notes

Notes

can be broken, and good habits can be learned and consciously established. The process of replacing a bad habit with a good one is frequently very difficult. Because we develop some habits almost unconsciously, pinpointing where change is needed can take much thought and effort. Our self-esteem is affected by our ability to develop good habits.

Facial expressions can be revealing. We all know people who constantly frown or others who frequently and easily smile. First, be aware of your own facial expressions, because they affect people's perceptions of you. A constant frown usually conveys problems, anxieties, and worries. At the same time, *don't read too much* into another person's facial expression. Observe it, but look for verification of it in actions and body language.

Procrastination is a bad habit. Put it off! Recognize that we avoid what we don't like or makes us uncomfortable, and understand that mental blocking is often caused by not knowing the details of how to do something. Even the smallest step starts the process and is often a catalyst to generating enthusiasm about the entire undertaking. When a project that you dread is facing you, immediately take one step—as small as it may be. That one step can remove the mental block that often leads to procrastination

Also, remember Plato's words, *"Well begun is half done."* Force yourself to take that first step.

Delegation is not a new idea. Leaders have always accomplished goals through the efforts of others. Delegation is not just a random distribution of work to be done. It requires not only an understanding of what needs to be done but also knowledge of the skills, abilities, and motivators of the potential doers. Delegating may or may not include instructions about how to complete the job, depending on the experience level of the doer, but it should always include an explanation of when and why the job needs to be done.

As time passes, check on the progress of the job without interfering or suggesting lack of confidence in the doer. Give him/her as much free reign as possible so that his/her innovative ideas can be free to surface.

Meetings are becoming an increasingly important activity in all areas of endeavor. Meetings come in many types, from information sharing, to brainstorming, to problem solving, to decision making. They may be chaired or facilitated. Meeting logistics also come in many varieties, from conference rooms to construction sites, to shop floors, etc. Meeting content encompasses the whole of existence—there has probably been a meeting on every topic we could suggest!

Notes

Notes

Whatever the type, logistics, or content, there are meeting fundamentals that are important for effective outcomes: (1) Agendas, detailing topics to be discussed with allotted times and presenters' names, and indicating the process to be used (e.g., brainstorming, decision making etc.) should be distributed a few days before the meeting. (2) Meetings should begin on time. (3) Agendas should be followed during the meeting. (4) Members should have the opportunity to participate and should be protected from personal attack, and (5) meetings should end as scheduled.

Anger is a powerful emotion that is seldom needed and should rarely be shown. Perhaps some situations involving safety could require an explosive response, but in normal circumstances, hostility usually backfires on the angry person. People view him/her as out of control, unable to be level headed. Rage can instill fear in others, causing diminished communication and productivity. People want to avoid a furious person; they don't want to be the receiver of an aggressive scolding.

Anger can become a bad habit. It can cloud perceptions and cause snap, shooting-from-the-hip judgments. Work to keep your temper under strict control. A clear, cool head can generate confidence and can be an **enabling** leadership trait.

Memory improvement is a frequent desire. A good memory for facts and names is an important leadership skill. You have heard of various methods and techniques for improving your memory. We suggest some very basic ones: (1) Concentrate and listen carefully—if, for example, an introduction is mumbled, ask to have the name repeated. (2) When trying to memorize numbers, work in number groups—most people can remember only six or seven in a string. (3) Make notes of key, memory-jogging words. (4) Try to associate a new fact with a familiar situation, and (5) develop and use your own acronyms. Never stop working to develop a keen memory. The following words of advice apply: "Use it, or lose it."

Focus/Concentration. . . We define "focus" as the ability to direct attention to a specific objective, situation, or problem requiring an answer or an action. The method of focusing is concentration. The leader needs to set the priorities on which concern is to be directed, thus focusing the efforts where they are likely to have the biggest payoff. This is an **energizing** action.

Symbolism. The environment abounds with symbolism. Symbols can evoke positive and negative reactions. Carpeting in the office, an impressive title, a genuine leather briefcase, a private

Notes

_____
_____
_____
_____
_____
_____
_____
_____
_____
_____
_____
_____
_____
_____
_____
_____
_____
_____
_____
_____
_____
_____
_____
_____
_____
_____

Notes

telephone can all be signs of success. A smaller office, steel as opposed to wood furniture, a shared telephone can represent diminished status. You need to be aware of symbolism, particularly if you are new to a group. Be careful not to destroy or diminish a symbol that others hold important; for doing so can quickly hurt morale and create resentment toward you.

Postscripts

In the Preface, we said that we were writing yet another book on leadership to fill what we saw as a void—a book that quickly and easily provides a condensed guide to effective leadership. It is you, the reader, that will determine whether or not we have succeeded.

It is our hope that as you read this book you found yourself nodding your head "yes" in agreement or even shaking it "no" in disagreement. In other words, we hope that you were actively involved and will continue to investigate and to practice leadership skills and traits. We hope the note sections are filled with your thoughts, reactions, and plans.

Many of the ideas and suggestions in this book receive much lip service but are often quickly pushed aside by time or cost considerations that seemingly are in conflict. We maintain that if a leader ignores our leadership suggestions, his/her leadership success is at risk of failing. In the long term, the skill and trait improvement suggestions presented herein enhance leadership success.

The prospects for the organization's success are also improved when its leaders' skills are

Notes

improved. Most organizations claim that their most important resource is their people. Improvement in the leaders' skills has to have a positive affect on the organization's success.

Leadership is ubiquitous in the sense that it's important in all human endeavors, not just the corporate world. Whatever the setting—sports, music, art, etc.—leaders are needed to envision, engage, enable, energize and enact. The Five Es apply across all diciplines.

To return to our metaphor of a toolbox, think of leadership skills and traits as the tools at your disposal. Work to make them the highest quality available, and ready for any situation.

Finally, remember that leadership is an interactive, living, on-going process. A challenge that will keep us occupied the rest of our lives!

> "The manager administers,
> the leader innovates.
> The manager relies on systems,
> the leader relies on people.
> The manager does things right,
> the leader does the right thing."
> *Fortune Magazine*

Notes

Suggested Readings

Belasco, James A. and Ralph C. Stayer, *Flight of the Buffalo: Soaring to Excellence, Learning to Let Employees Lead*, New York: Warner Books, 1994.

Bennis, Warren G., *On Becoming a Leader*, Reading, MA: Addison-Wesley Publishing Co., 1989.

Bennis, Warren G., *Leaders: Strategies for Taking Charge*, New York: HarperBusiness, 1997.

Blanchard, Kenneth, *Leadership and the One Minute Manager: Increasing Effectiveness Through Situational Leadership*, New York: William Morrow & Co., 1985.

Chapman, Elwood, *Your Attitude is Showing: A Primer of Human Relations*, Englewood Cliffs, NJ: Prentice Hall, 1996.

Covey, Stephen, *Principle-Centered Leadership*, New York: Simon & Schuster, 1992.

Covey, Stephen, *The Seven Habits of Highly Effective People*, New York: Simon & Schuster, 1989.

Notes

Dale Carnegie & Associates, Inc., Stuart R. Levine and Michael A. Crom, *The Leader in You*, New York: Simon & Schuster, 1993.

Daniels, Madeline Marie, *Realistic Leadership*, Englewood Cliffs, NJ: Prentice-Hall, 1983.

DePree, Max, *Leadership is an Art*, New York: Doubleday, 1989.

DePree, Max, *Leadership Jazz*, New York: Doubleday, 1992.

Drucker, Peter F., *The Effective Executive*, New York: HarperBusiness, 1967.

Drucker, Peter F., *Managing for the Future, The 1990s and Beyond*, New York: Penguin Group, 1992.

Dubrin, Andrew J., *10 Minute Guide to Effective Leadership*, New York: Macmillan, 1997.

Farson, Richard, *Management of the Absurd*, New York: Simon & Schuster, 1996.

Gardner, John W., *On Leadership*, New York: The Free Press (Division of Simon and Schuster), 1990.

Heifetz, Ronald A., *Leadership Without Easy Answers*, Cambridge, MA: Belknap, 1994.

Jaworski, Joseph and Betty S. Flowers, *Synchronicity: The Inner Path of Leadership*, San Francisco, CA: Berrett-Koehler Publishers Inc., 1998.

Kaltman, Al, *Cigars, Whiskey & Winning: Leadership Lessons from Ulysses S. Grant*, New York: Prentice Hall Trade, 1998.

Katzenbach, Jon R., *Teams at the Top: Unleashing the Potential of Both Teams and Individual Leaders*, Boston, MA: Harvard Business School, 1997.

Klopp, Hap, *The Adventure of Leadership: An Unorthodox Business Guide*, New York: Berkley Publishing, 1991.

Kotter, John P., *A Force for Change: How Leadership Differs from Management*, New York: The Free Press, 1990.

Kouzes, James and Barry Z. Posner, *The Leadership Challenge*, San Francisco: Jossey-Bass, 1987.

Maxwell, John C., *Developing the Leader Within You*, Nashville, TN: Thomas Nelson Inc., 1993.

Notes

Notes

Maxwell, John C., *The 21 Irrefutable Laws of Leadership: Follow Them and People Will Follow You*, Nashville, TN: Thomas Nelson Inc., 1998.

McCall, Morgan W., *High Flyers: Developing the Next Generation of Leaders*, Boston, MA: Harvard Business School, 1998.

McConnell, Taylor, *Group Leadership for Self-Realization*, New York: Mason & Lipscomb Publishers, Inc., 1993.

Nelson, Bob and Burton Morris, *1001 Ways to Energize Employees*, New York: Workman Publishing Co., 1997.

Oakley, Ed and Doug Krug, *Enlightened Leadership: Getting to the Heart of Change*, New York: Simon and Schuster, 1991.

Phillips, Donald T., *Lincoln on Leadership: Executive Strategies for Tough Times*, New York: Warner Books, 1993.

Quinlivan-Hall, David and Peter Renner, *In Search of Solutions: Sixty ways to guide your problemsolving group*, Vancouver, BC: PFR Training Associates Ltd., 1990.

Roberts, Wess, *Leadership Secrets of Attila the Hun*, New York: Warner Books, 1991.

Senge, Peter M., *The Fifth Discipline: The Art and Practice of the Learning Organization*, New York: Doubleday, 1994.

Slater, Robert, *Jack Welch and the GE Way: Management Insights and Leadership Secrets of the Legendary CEO*, New York: McGraw-Hill, 1998.

Slater, Robert, *Get Better or Get Beaten: 31 Leadership Secrets from GE's Jack Welch*, Burr Ridge, IL: Irwin Professional, 1996.

Southworth, Miles and Donna Southworth, *How to Implement Total Quality Management*, Livonia, NY: Graphic Arts Publishing Inc., 1992.

Tichy, Noel M., *The Leadership Engine: How Winning Companies Build Leaders at Every Level*, New York: HarperBusiness, 1997.

Wills, Garry, *Certain Trumpets: The Call of Leaders*, New York: Simon & Schuster, 1994.

Zigler, Zig, *See You at the Top*, Gretna, LA: Pelican Publishing Co., 1997.

Notes

Index

Barbara Birkett

Barbara Birkett is an Associate Professor at Rochester Institute of Technology's (RIT) School of Printing Management and Sciences where she teaches courses in personal leadership, economics of production management, financial controls, and estimating. She is Director of the school's newly-established Digital Publishing Center whose mission is to educate students in on-demand publishing and to develop unique on-demand publishing initiatives.

Recently Barbara completed ten years as the graduate coordinator for the master's degree in Graphic Arts Systems, a graduate program that combines management and technical courses.

Before coming to RIT, Barbara and her husband owned and operated a typesetting firm in Ann Arbor, Michigan. Prior to that, she worked for the then Michigan Bell Telephone Company where she held managerial positions ranging from business services manager, to central office chief operator, to staff assistant for budgeting for the Detroit metro area. Barbara also taught English and English literature at the secondary level.

Barbara holds an MBA in International Business from the University of Michigan, an MBA in Accounting from RIT, and a BA in English from Aquinas College in Michigan. She is a certified public accountant in the state of Maryland.

Warren Daum

Warren Daum has been active in the graphic arts industry for 35 years. He is best known as a "people person." He is a committed and ardent supporter of education and training as a prerequisite for leadership. He has been a mentor and advisor for a broad spectrum of people and is affectionately called "the printer's shrink."

Warren is a graduate of Brown University with a BS degree. During his undergraduate years he attended the Rhode Island School of Design as an avocation. He earned a MS degree in Psychology from Columbia University. The Navy sent him to the Harvard Business School. He served five years in the Navy during World War II and retired as Lt. Commander, U.S.N.R. Following his Navy career, Warren spent 20 years as chief executive officer and vice president of the Gravure Technical Association. He is past president and life trustee of the Gravure Education Foundation.

He has been associated with Rochester Institute of Technology (RIT) as advisor to the dean and an adjunct professor. He developed a course in the dynamics of leadership and enjoyed teaching the fundamentals of leadership for many years.

Daum has been a trustee of the National Scholarship Trust Fund and a member of the Society of Fellows of the Graphic Arts Technical Foundation (GATF). He has been a visiting professor and advisor to the dean of Nesbitt College of Design Arts of Drexel University. He has been honored as a life member of the European Gravure Association and is the American trustee of the Aller International Graphic Arts Foundation. He is an Honorary Professor and Nestor of the Graphic Arts Institute of Denmark.

A writer, lecturer, and advisor, Warren has served on many boards, including Western Michigan University, California Polytechnic University, and Arizona State University.

Miles Southworth

Miles Southworth is President of Graphic Arts Publishing Inc., a publisher of books and newsletters about graphic arts topics. He is editor of the *Ink on Paper* newsletter that deals with all aspects of imaging. Southworth is author of several books on quality and color reproduction, and a frequent consultant. He is Professor Emeritus from Rochester Institute of Technology's (RIT) School of Printing Management and Sciences. He was its director from 1985-1991. Before joining RIT, he worked in the printing industry.

Southworth consults with newspapers and magazine publishers, separators, printers, equipment manufacturers and universities internationally to improve color reproduction, quality and productivity. He participates in company training programs and plans curriculums. Southworth is a frequent speaker at conferences, seminars and workshops worldwide.

Professor Southworth is a contributing editor to *Printing Impressions* magazine. He and his wife, Donna, published a monthly tutorial newsletter, titled *The Quality Control Scanner,* for 14 years that dealt with quality and color improvement. They now publish the *Ink on Paper* newsletter. Southworth authored the book, *Color Separation Techniques,* 3rd ed. He and Donna co-authored the *Pocket Guide to Color Reproduction,* now in its 3rd edition, *Quality and Productivity in the Graphic Arts* and *How to Implement Total Quality Management.* With Thad McIlroy of Arcadia House, they also co-authored *The Color Resource Complete Color Glossary,* a definitive reference for correct usage of color prepress terminology. Miles and Donna's latest book is titled *Color Separation on the Desktop.* These books and newsletters are available from Graphic Arts Publishing, Livonia, NY.

Miles Southworth received his BS degree from the the University of Michigan and his MS degree from the University of Rochester. He is past president of the Technical Association of the Graphic Arts (TAGA), has served as chairman of the TAGA color committee and is presently the secretary-treasurer of TAGA. He is currently working with the Graphic Communications Association (GCA) to determine requirements for commercial printing.